MW00962768

HOME F   ED

SOUTHERN RECIPES

SWEETWATER
PRESS

Home Folks' Old-Fashioned Southern Recipes

Copyright © 2006 Sweetwater Press

Produced by Cliff Road Books

All rights reserved. No part of this book may be reproduced in any form or by any electronic or mechanical means, including information storage and retrieval systems, without written permission of the publisher.

The trademarked brand names used in some of the recipes of this book are integral to those recipes and do not represent endorsement by the brands or their owners.

While every effort has been made to ensure the accuracy of the recipes in this book, the publisher is not responsible for inaccuracies or less than satisfactory results. The publisher shall not be liable or responsible for any loss, injury, or damage allegedly arising from any information or suggestion in this book.

ISBN-13: 978-1-58173-639-7
ISBN-10: 1-58173-639-8

Design by Miles G. Parsons

Printed in China

HOME FOLKS' OLD-FASHIONED

SOUTHERN RECIPES

SWEETWATER
PRESS

CONTENTS

APPETIZERS

CHEESE STRAWS

1/2 cup butter, softened
16 ounces sharp cheddar cheese, shredded
2 cups flour
salt, to taste
1 teaspoon cayenne pepper

Combine butter, cheese, salt, flour, and cayenne pepper in bowl; mix well. Spoon into pastry bag. Press straws onto a nonstick baking sheet. Bake at 350° for 7 minutes. Makes about 100 cheese straws.

SAUSAGE BALLS

1 pound sausage
1/3 cup bread crumbs
1 egg, beaten
1/2 cup ketchup
2 tablespoons brown sugar
1 tablespoon soy sauce
1 tablespoon vinegar

Combine sausage, bread crumbs, and egg in a bowl; mix well. Shape into small balls. In a skillet over low heat, brown the balls on all sides; drain. Combine the ketchup, brown sugar, soy sauce, and vinegar; mix well and pour over sausage balls. Simmer for 15 to 20 minutes.

PIMENTO CHEESE

1-1/2 cups mayonnaise
1 (4-ounce) jar pimentos, drained
1 teaspoon grated onion
1/2 teaspoon salt
1/4 teaspoon cayenne pepper
2 cups sharp cheddar cheese, shredded

In a large bowl, combine mayonnaise, pimentos, onion, salt, and cayenne pepper; mix thoroughly. Add cheddar cheese and stir to combine.

DEVILED EGGS

6 hard-boiled eggs, peeled and cut in halves
3 tablespoons mayonnaise
1 tablespoon sweet pickle relish
1 tablespoon mustard
salt and pepper, to taste
paprika

Remove yolks from eggs, leaving the whites intact. In a bowl, combine yolks and mayonnaise; mix until smooth. Add relish, mustard, salt, and pepper; stir to combine. Spoon yolk mixture into the egg whites and sprinkle with paprika.

BOILED PEANUTS

3 quarts water
1/2 cup salt
2 pounds fresh, raw peanuts, in shells

Put the water and salt in a large stockpot; bring to a boil. Add the peanuts and simmer for at least 1 hour, until peanuts are tender. Drain and serve.

TEXAS CAVIAR

2 cups black-eyed peas
1 cup olive oil
1/4 cup red wine vinegar
1 tablespoon garlic, minced
1 teaspoon salt
1/2 teaspoon black pepper
1/2 teaspoon hot sauce
1 tablespoon sugar
1 tomato, chopped
1 green bell pepper, finely chopped
1 onion, thinly sliced

Put the peas in a large saucepan and cover with water. Bring to a boil, cover, and cook until peas are tender but firm. Drain. In a large bowl, combine the olive oil, vinegar, garlic, salt, pepper, hot sauce, and sugar; stir well to combine. Stir in peas, tomato, bell pepper, and onion. Refrigerate for 24 hours, stirring occasionally.

FRIED DILL PICKLES

2 eggs, beaten
1 cup milk
1 tablespoon Worcestershire sauce
hot sauce
3/4 teaspoon cayenne pepper
1/4 teaspoon salt
1/4 teaspoon garlic powder
2 cups cornmeal
1 cup flour
1 teaspoon salt
3/4 teaspoon pepper
1 quart sliced dill pickles, drained
vegetable oil, for frying
salt and pepper, to taste

In a mixing bowl, combine the eggs, milk, Worcestershire sauce, hot sauce, cayenne pepper, salt, and garlic powder; mix thoroughly. In another bowl, combine cornmeal, flour, salt, and pepper. Dip pickles into egg wash then dredge in flour mixture. Deep fry in vegetable oil until golden brown. Drain. Season with salt and pepper.

CRAB DIP

1 pound lump crab meat
1 cup mayonnaise
1/2 cup onions, finely chopped
2 garlic cloves, minced
1 cup cheddar cheese, shredded
2 tablespoons Worcestershire sauce
2 tablespoons lemon juice
1 teaspoon salt
1 teaspoon pepper
crackers

In a shallow baking dish, combine all ingredients except crackers. Bake at 325° for about 40 minutes. Serve with crackers.

PICKLED BEETS AND EGGS

1 (16-ounce) can sliced beets, drained, liquid reserved
1/2 cup sugar
1/2 cup cider vinegar
6 whole black peppercorns
6 whole allspice berries
6 hard-boiled eggs, shelled
1 small onion, sliced

Combine reserved beet liquid, sugar, vinegar, peppercorns, and allspice in a medium saucepan. Bring to a boil over medium heat, stirring until sugar dissolves; remove from heat. Add eggs and onion and turn to coat completely. Add beets. Cover pan and refrigerate until eggs are deep pink color, turning occasionally, about 8 hours.

Drain juices. Cut eggs lengthwise in half. Arrange beets and onion on plate. Top with eggs and serve.

SPICED PECANS

1/2 cup light brown sugar
1/2 cup white sugar
1/2 teaspoon cinnamon
1/4 teaspoon ground cloves
1/2 cup water
2 cups pecan halves

Mix together all ingredients except pecans. Boil until a few drops of syrup hardens as soon as dropped in a little ice water. Remove from heat and add pecans. Stir until the mixture begins to thicken and nuts are evenly coated. Pour onto wax paper and break apart into small pieces.

STUFFED CELERY

3 celery stalks
3 ounces cream cheese
1 tablespoon pimento stuffed green olives, chopped
1 tablespoon onion, chopped
1 tablespoon sweet pickle relish
1 tablespoon pecans, chopped
1-1/2 teaspoons mayonnaise

Wash celery and cut into 3-inch pieces. Combine remaining ingredients and mix well. Stuff celery pieces with the mixture.

CHEESE BALL

2 (8-ounce) packages cream cheese
8 ounces processed cheese spread
3/4 cup pecans, chopped
1 (8-1/2-ounce) can crushed pineapple, well drained
1/3 cup green bell pepper, finely chopped
3 tablespoons onion, chopped
1/2 tablespoon seasoned salt
1/2 teaspoon garlic powder
cayenne pepper, to taste
crackers

Combine cream cheese and processed cheese spread; mix well. Stir in 1/2 cup pecans, pineapple, and next 5 ingredients. Chill. Form mixture into 1 or 2 balls and roll in remaining pecans. Serve with crackers.

HAM DIP

2 (4-1/2-ounce) cans deviled ham
1 (12-ounce) package cream cheese
2 tablespoons Worcestershire sauce
1/8 teaspoon cayenne pepper
1/3 cup green bell pepper, finely chopped
1/3 cup red bell pepper, finely chopped

Combine ham, cream cheese, Worcestershire sauce, and cayenne pepper. Stir until well combined. Stir in bell pepper. Refrigerate for 1 hour before serving.

SOUPS

CORN CHOWDER

2 cups chicken, cooked and chopped
1 (10-ounce) can potato soup
1 (10-ounce) can cream of chicken soup
1 (10-ounce) can corn
1-1/2 cups milk
1 cup chicken broth
1/3 cup sliced green onions
1-1/2 cups cheddar cheese, shredded

Combine chicken, canned soups, corn, milk, chicken broth, and green onions in a saucepan; mix well. Cook over medium heat for 5 to 8 minutes or until heated through, stirring constantly. Remove from heat. Add cheese and continue stirring until melted. Makes 8 servings.

BLACK-EYED PEA SOUP

1 pound dried black-eyed peas
2 strips bacon, diced
1 onion, finely chopped
6 cups chicken broth
1 tablespoon Worcestershire sauce
1 (14-ounce) can tomatoes
1 teaspoon hot sauce
salt and pepper, to taste
1 teaspoon brown sugar

Place peas in a large pot and cover with water; bring to a boil. Cook until beans are tender, about 1 hour. Remove from heat and drain.

In a stockpot, brown the bacon over medium heat. Remove bacon and drain. Pour off all but 1 tablespoon of rendered bacon fat. Add onion and sauté until translucent, about 6 minutes. Add peas, cooked bacon, chicken broth, and Worcestershire sauce. Bring to a boil. Add the rest of the ingredients and cook for 10 more minutes.

VEGETABLE SOUP

4 tablespoons olive oil
1 large onion, chopped
2 garlic cloves, minced
2 cups zucchini, diced
2 cups squash, sliced
1 green bell pepper, chopped
2 cups potatoes, cubed
2 cups carrots, sliced
2 cups green beans, trimmed
8 cups vegetable or chicken broth
1 ear of corn, kernels removed
1 can baby peas, drained
2 (14-ounce) cans tomatoes
salt and pepper, to taste
1/2 teaspoon dried oregano

In a large pot, sauté the onion and garlic in olive oil over medium-low heat. Cook until onion is translucent, about 6 minutes. Add the zucchini, squash, bell pepper, potatoes, carrots, and green beans; cook, stirring occasionally, for 5 minutes.

Add the broth and increase heat to high. Bring to a simmer and add corn, peas, tomatoes, and seasonings. Reduce the heat to low and cover. Cook until vegetables are tender, about 25 to 30 minutes.

OYSTER SOUP

1 pint oysters
2 tablespoons butter
1 cup onion, chopped
salt and pepper, to taste
1/2 teaspoon garlic powder
4 cups heavy cream
2 tablespoons parsley, finely chopped

Drain oysters in a colander and reserve liquor. In a large saucepan, melt the butter. Add the onion and sauté until tender. Add oyster liquor, garlic powder, salt, and pepper, and simmer for 15 minutes. Add oysters and cook until the edges begin to curl, about 1 to 2 minutes. Add cream, but do not allow to boil. Garnish with chopped parsley.

HAMBURGER SOUP

1 pound ground beef
1 onion, chopped
1 garlic clove, minced
8 cups beef broth
1 cup green beans, trimmed
1 cup baby peas
1 cup carrots, sliced
1 can cream-style corn
2 (14-ounce) cans tomatoes
salt and pepper, to taste

In a large skillet, sauté ground chuck, onion, and garlic until meat is brown. Drain and transfer to a large stockpot. Add remaining ingredients. Bring to a boil; reduce heat and simmer for 45 minutes or until vegetables are tender.

RABBIT STEW

1 rabbit, cut into 6 to 8 pieces
2 cups buttermilk
4 slices bacon, diced
1 cup flour
1 teaspoon salt
1/2 teaspoon pepper
1 large onion, diced
2 garlic cloves, minced
1/2 cup apple cider
1 cup corn
2 large potatoes, cubed
1/4 teaspoon cayenne pepper
4 cups chicken stock
2 cups fresh tomatoes, chopped

In a large dish, combine rabbit and buttermilk. Refrigerate and allow to soak for at least 2 hours.

In a stockpot, brown the bacon over medium heat. Remove bacon and drain.

In another dish, mix flour, salt, and pepper together. Dredge rabbit in flour mixture and brown in bacon drippings. Remove rabbit pieces and set aside. Add onion and cook about 5 minutes. Add garlic and cook for 1 more minute. Pour in apple cider and reduce by half, scraping the bottom of the stockpot to release any brown bits. Return rabbit to stockpot along with bacon, corn, potatoes, cayenne pepper, and chicken stock. Bring to a boil. Reduce heat and simmer for 1-1/2 hours. Add the tomatoes and simmer for 1 more hour.

POTATO SOUP

4 tablespoons butter
1/2 cup onion, finely chopped
2 tablespoons flour
4 cups potatoes, peeled and cubed
3 cups milk
1/2 cup chicken broth
salt and pepper, to taste

In a large saucepan, melt the butter over medium heat. Add the onion and cook until soft, about 5 minutes. Whisk in the flour and cook for 1 minute. Add the potatoes, milk, and chicken broth. Cook until potatoes are tender, about 15 minutes. Season with salt and pepper.

BEAN SOUP

3 tablespoons olive oil
1-1/2 cups ham, chopped
1 cup onion, chopped
1 cup celery, chopped
6 cups chicken broth
1 pound great Northern beans, soaked overnight and drained
1 teaspoon garlic salt
2 teaspoons salt
3/4 teaspoon black pepper

In a large stockpot, heat olive oil over medium heat. Sauté ham, onion, and celery for about 5 minutes, or until onion and celery are tender. Add chicken broth and beans. Bring to a simmer, reduce heat to low, cover, and cook for 2 hours. About 20 minutes before cooking time is up, add seasonings.

BROCCOLI SOUP

1 bunch broccoli
1/4 cup butter
1 medium onion, chopped
celery
2 cups milk
1 (10-1/2 ounce) can cream of chicken soup
2 cups chicken broth
cheddar cheese, shredded
salt and pepper, to taste

Sauté the broccoli, butter, onion, and celery until tender. Stir in milk, chicken soup, and broth. Add the cheese and cook on low heat to melt. Do not boil. Season with salt and pepper.

SPLIT PEA SOUP WITH BACON AND ROSEMARY

4 bacon slices, chopped
1 small onion, chopped
1 medium leek, sliced
1 large carrot, peeled and chopped
2 garlic cloves, minced
4 (14-1/2-ounce) cans low-salt chicken broth
1/4 cups green split peas, rinsed
2 bay leaves
1/2 teaspoon fresh rosemary, chopped

Sauté bacon in a heavy pot over medium-high heat until crisp and brown. Add onion, leek, carrot, and garlic and sauté until vegetables begin to soften, about 6 minutes. Add broth, peas, bay leaves, and rosemary; bring soup to a boil. Reduce heat to medium-low, cover, and simmer until peas are tender, stirring occasionally, about 1 hour. Season soup to taste with salt and pepper. Makes 4 to 6 servings.

CABBAGE SOUP

3 tablespoons olive oil
1 onion, chopped
1/2 red bell pepper, minced
2 garlic cloves, minced
2 tablespoons balsamic vinegar
1 teaspoon sugar
3 cups cabbage, shredded
1 large tomato, finely chopped
6 cups beef stock or chicken broth
1 teaspoon salt
1 teaspoon garlic powder
1/2 teaspoon black pepper

In a stockpot, heat the olive oil over medium heat. Sauté the onion and bell pepper until onion is translucent, about 6 minutes. Add the garlic and cook for 1 more minute. Add the balsamic vinegar and sugar and bring to a simmer. Stir in the cabbage. Add the tomato, broth, and seasonings. Simmer, uncovered, for 30 to 40 minutes, or until cabbage is tender.

FROGMORE STEW

1-1/2 gallons water
2 tablespoons salt
2 tablespoons pepper
1 tablespoon celery seed
2 bay leaves
1 teaspoon dry mustard
2 teaspoons sweet paprika
1/2 teaspoon mace
1 teaspoon ground cardamom
2 pounds red potatoes
2 pounds spicy smoked sausage, cut into 2-inch pieces
10 ears corn, husk removed and cut into 3-inch pieces
4 pounds shrimp

In a large stockpot, combine water, salt, pepper, celery seed, bay leaves, dry mustard, sweet paprika, mace, and cardamom. Bring to a boil. Add potatoes and cook 15 minutes. Stir in the sausage and cook for 5 minutes. Add corn and cook for 5 more minutes. Add the shrimp and cook 5 more minutes, or until shrimp turn pink. Drain.

SHE-CRAB SOUP

1 tablespoon butter
1 onion, finely chopped
1/2 tablespoon flour
2 cups fish stock
2 cups milk
1/2 cup heavy cream
1/2 teaspoon salt
1/4 teaspoon pepper
1 pound crab meat, cooked and picked over
1/2 cup crab roe
paprika
fresh parsley, chopped

In a stockpot, melt butter over medium heat. Add onion and sauté for 2 minutes. Slowly whisk in flour, stirring until it dissolves. Pour in the stock and whisk until combined. Gradually add the milk, heavy cream, salt, pepper, crab meat, and roe. Cook, stirring frequently, for about 20 minutes. Garnish with paprika and parsley.

Tomato Soup

1 quart canned tomatoes, chopped
1 teaspoon butter
pepper
2 teaspoons sugar
3 teaspoons flour
1 cup milk

Mix tomatoes and butter, sprinkle with pepper. Cook in a saucepan until it starts to boil, stirring occasionally. Mix sugar, flour, and milk together; stir well. Pour into boiling tomatoes. Reduce heat and simmer for a few minutes, stirring occasionally.

Chili Con Carne

2 tablespoons vegetable oil
1/2 cup onion, thinly sliced
1/2 cup green bell pepper, diced
1 garlic clove, crushed
3/4 pound ground beef
3/4 cup boiling water
1 (20-ounce) can tomatoes
1 to 2 tablespoons chili powder
1/8 teaspoon paprika
salt
2 cups canned kidney beans

Heat oil in a large stockpot. Cook onion, green pepper, and garlic about 10 minutes. Add meat. Increase heat; stir until meat is brown. Add water, tomatoes, chili powder, paprika, and a little salt. Cover and cook over low heat about 45 minutes. Add beans. Cook 30 minutes. Adjust seasoning to taste before servings. Makes 4 to 5 servings.

CHICKEN AND SAUSAGE GUMBO

3 to 4 chicken breasts halves, cut in small chunks
4 chicken thighs, trimmed and cut in small pieces
1/2 teaspoon Creole seasoning blend
3 tablespoons flour
1 tablespoon vegetable oil
2 cups smoked sausage, cut in 1/2-inch pieces
1/2 cup vegetable oil
1/2 cup all-purpose flour
1 cup onion, chopped
1/2 cup green bell pepper, chopped
1/4 cup red bell pepper, chopped
3 ribs celery, chopped
3 medium garlic cloves, minced
1 (14-1/2-ounce) can diced tomatoes
1 small bay leaf
6 cups chicken broth
1 teaspoon Creole seasoning blend, or to taste
1/2 teaspoon dried thyme leaves
salt and freshly ground black pepper to taste
4 green onions, chopped
2 tablespoons fresh parsley, chopped

Cut chicken into small pieces; sprinkle with Creole seasoning then toss with flour. Heat 1 tablespoon oil in a heavy skillet over medium heat; add chicken. Cook, stirring, until browned. Transfer to a dish and set aside. Brown sliced sausage; add to chicken mixture.

In a heavy pot, heat 1/2 cup oil; add 1/2 cup flour. Cook, stirring constantly, until the roux reaches a deep blonde-color, about the color of dark peanut butter. You can do this over medium to medium-high heat, but stir constantly and watch carefully. When roux has reached the color you want, add the vegetables and stir briskly. Continue to cook, stirring constantly, for about 3 to 4 minutes.

Add the chicken broth, seasonings, chicken, and sausage. Bring to a boil, then cook for about 1 to 1-1/2 hours, skimming excess fat off the top several times, as needed. Add the chopped green onions and parsley; heat for 5 to 10 minutes longer. Mound hot cooked rice in bowls, ladle the gumbo around the mound. Serve with crusty bread and butter. Makes 6 servings.

BEEF STEW

1/4 cup butter
2 onions, chopped
3 celery stalks, chopped
1 pound sirloin tips
3 potatoes, sliced
1 package baby carrots
1 (15-ounce) can English peas, drained
4 cups beef broth
1 teaspoon garlic powder
salt and pepper

Melt butter over medium heat in a large saucepan. Add onions and celery and cook until tender. Add sirloin strips; cook stirring frequently until browned. Add remaining ingredients and cook over low heat for 30 to 35 minutes.

CHEDDAR CHEESE SOUP

1 medium onion, chopped
1 cup celery, chopped
1/4 cup butter
1/4 cup flour
3/4 teaspoon dry mustard
2 teaspoons Worcestershire sauce
2 cups chicken broth
2 medium carrots, chopped
3 cups potatoes, chopped
1/2 pound smoked sausage, cut into 1/4-inch cubes
3 cups milk
3 cups shredded sharp cheddar cheese
salt and pepper, to taste

Sauté onion and celery in butter until soft. Stir in flour, mustard, and Worcestershire sauce. Cook, stirring, 2 minutes or until vegetables are evenly coated and mixture is bubbly. Stir in broth, carrots, potatoes, and sausage. Bring to a boil. Lower heat; cover and simmer, stirring occasionally, 45 minutes or until potatoes and carrots are tender. Add milk. Cook over medium heat until almost boiling. Do not boil. Reduce heat to low; stir in cheese until melted. Add salt and pepper, if desired.

SALADS

OLD-FASHIONED FRUIT SALAD

1 (15-ounce) can pineapple chunks
1 can sliced peaches
2 apples, chopped
2 oranges, peeled and chopped
2 bananas, sliced
1 cup grapes
1 cup miniature marshmallows
1/2 cup sugar

Combine all ingredients. Mix well and refrigerate. Serve cold.

CHICKEN SALAD

1 (2-1/2 to 3-pound) chicken, cooked and coarsely chopped
2 cups celery, chopped
1/4 cup green bell pepper, chopped
1 cup sweet pickle relish
6 hard-boiled eggs, peeled and chopped
1-1/2 cups mayonnaise
1 teaspoon fresh lemon juice

Combine chicken, celery, green bell pepper, relish, and eggs in a bowl. Add mayonnaise and lemon juice; mix gently. Chill until ready to serve. Makes 8 servings.

Chicken Fruit Salad

1 orange, peeled, seeded, and sliced
15 large seedless grapes, halved
1/2 cup crushed pineapple, drained
1 banana, sliced
1 apple, diced
3 cups white chicken meat, cooked and diced
1 cup mayonnaise
lettuce

Mix all ingredients lightly but thoroughly. Chill and serve on lettuce.

Tuna Salad

1 (7-ounce) can tuna, drained
1/3 cup dill pickle, chopped
salt and pepper, to taste
1/4 teaspoon mustard
2 tablespoons mayonnaise

In a large bowl, combine all ingredients. Mix well.

Shrimp Salad

1 pound shrimp, cooked, peeled, and minced
3 hard-boiled eggs, peeled and finely chopped
2 cups celery, minced
1/2 cup mayonnaise
salt and pepper, to taste

In a large bowl combine shrimp, eggs, celery, and mayonnaise; mix well. Add salt and pepper and stir to combine.

Broccoli Salad

2 bunches broccoli, chopped
1 cup cheddar cheese, shredded
1 onion, sliced
1 cup mayonnaise
1/4 cup sugar
1/4 cup apple cider vinegar

Toss together the broccoli, cheese, and onion. In another bowl, combine the mayonnaise, sugar, and apple cider vinegar. Pour over broccoli mixture.

COLESLAW

1 large head cabbage, shredded
1 large green bell pepper, chopped
1 large purple onion, thinly sliced into rings
2/3 cup celery, chopped
1 (4-ounce) jar chopped pimentos, drained
1 cup sugar
3/4 cup oil
1 cup light vinegar
1 teaspoon dry mustard
2 teaspoons sugar
2 teaspoons dillweed
2 teaspoons parsley flakes
paprika, to taste
1 tablespoon salt

Combine cabbage, green bell pepper, onion, celery, and pimentos in a large bowl. Sprinkle with 1 cup sugar. Combine oil, vinegar, dry mustard, 2 teaspoons sugar, dillweed, parsley flakes, paprika, and salt in a saucepan. Bring to a rolling boil. Pour over cabbage mixture. Chill, covered, for 4 hours to overnight. Toss before serving. Makes 16 servings.

THREE BEAN SALAD

1 (1-pound) can cut green beans
1 (1-pound) can cut yellow wax beans
1 (1-pound) can red kidney beans
1/4 cup green pepper, chopped
1 medium onion, sliced very thin
1/2 cup cider vinegar
1/3 cup cooking oil
1/2 cup sugar
1 teaspoon salt
1 teaspoon pepper

Drain beans, rinse well, drain again. Add green peppers and sliced onion to beans. Mix together the rest of the ingredients and pour over beans.

OLD-FASHIONED POTATO SALAD

4 potatoes, peeled, cooked, and mashed
salt and pepper, to taste
1 cup mayonnaise
1/2 cup dill pickle, finely chopped
1/2 cup onion, finely chopped
3 hard-boiled eggs, peeled and finely chopped
2 tablespoons mustard
paprika

Combine mashed potatoes, salt, pepper, and mayonnaise. Stir in dill pickle, onion, eggs, and mustard. Mix well. Garnish with paprika.

Macaroni Salad

1 pound macaroni
1 bell pepper, finely chopped
1 onion, finely chopped
4 carrots, grated
1 can sweetened condensed milk
1/2 cup vinegar
1/2 cup sugar
1 cup mayonnaise

Cook macaroni and drain. Mix ingredients together. Marinate overnight.

Green Bean Salad

2 pounds green beans, cut to 2-inch length
juice of 1 lemon
1 tablespoon sugar
dash of pepper
1 onion, chopped
2 tablespoons mayonnaise

Cook the beans in salted water and drain. Mix the rest of the ingredients together, then add the beans.

CARROT SALAD

2 pounds carrots, sliced
1 small green bell pepper, cut in strips
1 small onion, thinly sliced
1 (10-1/2-ounce) can tomato soup, undiluted
1/4 cup salad oil
1 cup sugar
3/4 cup white vinegar
1 teaspoon mustard
1 teaspoon Worcestershire sauce
salt and pepper, to taste

Cook carrots in salted water until fork tender. Drain and cool. Mix together the rest of the ingredients, then add cooked carrots.

STRAWBERRY PINEAPPLE SALAD

1 package strawberry-flavored gelatin
1 (12-ounce) can crushed pineapple
2 cups cottage cheese
1 large container whipped topping
1 cup nuts

Put dry gelatin and crushed pineapple in a saucepan. Bring to a hard boil, then cool. Add cottage cheese, whipped topping, and nuts. Refrigerate several hours or overnight.

Pistachio Salad

1 (3-1/2-ounce) package pistachio instant pudding mix
1 (20-ounce) can crushed pineapple, undrained
1 cup miniature marshmallows
1/2 cup maraschino cherries, chopped
1/2 cup pecans, chopped
10 ounces whipped topping

Mix dry pudding with pineapple, marshmallows, cherries, and pecans.
Fold in whipped topping. Chill at least 1 hour before serving.

Spinach Salad

2 cups raw spinach
1/4 cup celery, chopped
1/4 cup onion, chopped
1/2 cup sharp cheddar cheese, shredded
1/4 teaspoon vinegar
1/2 cup mayonnaise
2 hard-boiled eggs, peeled and sliced

Wash spinach and pat dry with paper towels. Mix celery, onions,
cheese, vinegar, and mayonnaise. Pour dressing over spinach and toss.
Add sliced eggs.

COPPER PENNY SALAD

2 pounds cooked carrots, sliced
1 small onion, chopped
1 (10-1/2-ounce) can tomato soup, undiluted
1/2 cup salad oil
1 cup sugar
3/4 cup vinegar
1 teaspoon mustard

Combine all ingredients. Marinate overnight in the refrigerator and serve cold.

CABBAGE SALAD

1 pint vinegar
2 cups sugar
2 tablespoons salt
3/4 teaspoon celery seed
3/4 teaspoon mustard seed
1/3 teaspoon turmeric
8 cups cabbage, chopped
3 onions, chopped
3 green bell peppers, chopped

Combine vinegar, sugar, salt, celery seed, mustard seed, and turmeric in a saucepan and heat until just before boiling point. Pour over vegetables and put in jars. May be served immediately or can be jarred and kept in the refrigerator for months.

BREADS

Buttermilk Biscuits

1 cup self-rising flour
1 teaspoon sugar
1/4 cup shortening
1/2 cup buttermilk
1 to 2 tablespoons margarine, softened

Sift flour into a bowl; add sugar. Cut in shortening until crumbly. Add buttermilk; mix well. Roll or pat to 1/2-inch thickness on floured surface. Cut with biscuit cutter. Arrange on a greased baking sheet. Brush with margarine. Let stand for 5 to 10 minutes. Bake at 450° for 10 minutes or until golden brown. Serve hot. Makes 7 servings.

Dinner Rolls

3-1/2 cups all purpose flour
1 teaspoon salt
2 tablespoons sugar
2 tablespoons shortening
1 cup warm water
1 package dry yeast
melted butter

In a large bowl, sift together flour, salt, and sugar. Cut in shortening, and mix well to combine. Combine water and yeast, then add to flour mixture. Pour dough onto a floured surface and knead for several minutes. Let rise until dough doubles in size, about 1-1/2 hours. Pour out onto a floured surface and knead for several more minutes. Roll into small balls and let rise for another 1-1/2 hours, or until the dough doubles in size again. Brush tops of rolls with melted butter and bake at 375° until brown, about 10 to 15 minutes.

CORNBREAD

1-1/2 cups self-rising cornmeal
1/2 cup self-rising flour
1/4 cup vegetable oil
2 eggs, beaten
1/2 cup red bell pepper, chopped
2 jalapeño peppers, chopped
1 bunch green onions, chopped
1/2 cup whole kernel corn
3/4 to 1 cup buttermilk

Combine the cornmeal, flour, oil, and eggs in a bowl; mix well. Add red pepper, jalapeño peppers, green onions, corn, and enough buttermilk to make a batter of desired consistency. Pour into a well greased preheated cast-iron skillet or cornstick molds. Bake at 400° for 30 minutes or until golden brown. Makes 10 servings.

CORNBREAD MUFFINS

2 cups self-rising cornmeal mix
1/4 cup canola oil
1 tablespoon sugar
1 egg
1-1/4 cups milk

In a large bowl, combine all ingredients and mix well. Pour batter into a greased muffin pan. Bake at 425° until golden brown, about 20 to 25 minutes.

BLUEBERRY MUFFINS

1 cup sugar
1/2 cup butter
1 egg
1/4 teaspoon baking soda
1 teaspoon cream of tartar
2 cups flour
1/2 cup milk
2 cups blueberries

Cream sugar and butter. Add egg and beat well. Sift dry ingredients and add alternatively with milk. Fold in blueberries. Bake in muffin tins using muffin liners. Bake at 350° for 30 minutes. Makes 18 muffins.

BANANA BREAD

1/3 cup oil
1 cup sugar
3 eggs
1-2/3 cup Bisquick
1-1/2 cups ripe bananas, mashed
1/2 cup nuts, chopped
1/2 teaspoon vanilla

Beat all ingredients in an electric mixer for about 30 seconds. Bake at 350° until toothpick comes out clean. Cool for 5 minutes. Remove from pan.

PUMPKIN BREAD

3-1/2 cups flour
3 cups sugar
2 teaspoons baking soda
1/2 teaspoon salt
1 teaspoon nutmeg
1 teaspoon ground cloves
1 teaspoon allspice
1/2 teaspoon ginger
1 teaspoon cinnamon
1 cup canola oil
4 eggs, slightly beaten
1 cup water
2 cups pumpkin
1 cup dates, chopped
1 cup pecans, chopped
2 teaspoons powdered sugar

In a large bowl, sift together flour, sugar, baking soda, salt, nutmeg, cloves, allspice, ginger, and cinnamon. In another bowl, combine oil, eggs, and water. Combine the two mixtures and mix thoroughly. Add pumpkin, dates, and pecans; stir to combine. Pour into a greased cake pan and bake at 325° for 1 hour. Sprinkle with powdered sugar before serving.

BANANA-NUT BREAD

1-2/3 cups sugar
2/3 cups margarine, softened
2 eggs
1 teaspoon vanilla extract
2-1/2 cups flour
1-1/4 teaspoons baking powder
1-1/4 teaspoons baking soda
1 teaspoon salt
1/3 cup buttermilk
3 bananas, mashed
1 cup pecans, crushed

Cream sugar and margarine in a bowl until light and fluffy. Beat in eggs one at a time. Add vanilla. Sift dry ingredients together. Add to creamed mixture alternately with buttermilk, mixing well after each addition. Add bananas; mix well. Stir in pecans. Pour into two large greased loaf pans. Bake at 350° for 1 hour or until loaves test done. Remove from pans and let cool on wire racks. Makes 24 servings.

SOURDOUGH BREAD

1 cup sourdough starter
3 tablespoons cooking oil
1/2 teaspoon salt
1 package dry yeast
1/2 cup lukewarm water
2 or more cups flour
butter

Mix starter, oil, and salt in a large mixing bowl. Mix yeast and warm water. Add to mixture. Add flour to make stiff dough (you may use half whole wheat flour). Knead in bowl until smooth. Let rise until doubled in size. Place on board and knead, then shape into loaf. Place in greased loaf pan. Allow to rise, covering with wet cloth until doubled. Bake 350° for 30 minutes. Remove from pan and butter top.

MONKEY BREAD

4 cans buttermilk biscuits, quartered
cinnamon and sugar mixture
walnuts
1-1/2 cup butter
1 cup brown sugar

Divide biscuit dough into 16 biscuits, put in a bag with cinnamon sugar mixture and shake. Place in a well greased and floured Bundt pan, throwing in walnuts. In a saucepan, melt the butter. Add the brown sugar and cook until melted, stirring frequently. Pour over biscuits in pan. Bake at 350° for 35 minutes. Cool for 10 minutes, then remove.

SWEET POTATO BREAD

3 cups sugar
1 cup oil
4 eggs, beaten
2 cups sweet potatoes
3-1/2 cups all-purpose flour
1 teaspoon baking powder
2 teaspoons baking soda
2 teaspoons salt
2 teaspoons ground cloves
1 teaspoon cinnamon
1 teaspoon allspice
1 teaspoon nutmeg
1 cup raisins
2/3 cup water

Combine sugar, oil, and eggs. Add sweet potatoes and mix well. Combine dry ingredients and add to sweet potato mixture. Add raisins and water. Beat well. Pour into two greased loaf pans. Bake at 350° for 1 hour.

HUSH PUPPIES

1-1/2 cups cornmeal
1/2 cup flour
1/2 teaspoon baking soda
1 teaspoon salt
1/2 onion, chopped
1 cup buttermilk
1 egg
vegetable oil, for frying

In a large bowl, combine the cornmeal, flour, baking soda, salt, and onion; mix well. In another bowl, whisk together buttermilk and egg; add to dry ingredients. Heat oil in a large pot with deep sides. Drop batter by teaspoonfuls into the hot oil. Fry in batches until golden brown, about 2 minutes. Drain.

CRACKLIN' BREAD

2 cups cornmeal
1 teaspoon salt
1 teaspoon baking soda
1/2 teaspoon baking powder
1 cup buttermilk
1 egg, beaten
1 cup pork cracklings

In a large bowl, combine cornmeal, salt, soda, and baking powder. Add buttermilk, egg, and cracklings; mix well. Pour into a greased iron skillet and bake at 400° for 25 to 30 minutes, or until brown.

Johnny Cake

3 cups cornmeal
1 cup flour
pinch of salt
1 teaspoon baking soda
1 cup buttermilk
1/3 cup molasses

In a large bowl combine cornmeal, flour, and salt. In a small bowl, mix baking soda with buttermilk and molasses. Add to dry ingredients. Mix thoroughly. Pour into a greased iron skillet and bake at 400° for 25 to 30 minutes, or until brown.

Popovers

1 cup all-purpose flour
1/4 teaspoon salt
3/4 cup milk
2 eggs, beaten
1/2 teaspoon butter, melted

Sift together flour and salt in a mixer bowl. Add the milk gradually while stirring to make a paste. Add the eggs to the batter. Add the melted butter. Fill muffin tins two-thirds full, and bake at 450° for 10 minutes. Lower the heat to 350° and bake 30 minutes longer.

CHEESE BISCUITS

2 cups flour
1 tablespoon double-acting baking powder
1 teaspoon sugar
1/2 teaspoon salt
1/3 cup grated cheddar cheese
5 tablespoons butter, cut into small pieces
1 tablespoon grated Parmesan cheese
3/4 cup milk
paprika

In a large mixing bowl, sift together the flour, baking powder, sugar, and salt. Add cheddar cheese, butter, and Parmesan cheese. Add milk and stir just enough to make a soft, smooth dough. Turn the dough out onto a floured surface, and knead it for a few seconds. Sprinkle the dough with a little flour, and roll it out to 1/3-inch thickness. Cut out small biscuits with a biscuit cutter. Arrange biscuits on a baking sheet about 1-inch apart. Bake at 400° for 12 to 15 minutes or until golden brown. Sprinkle tops of biscuits with paprika.

TEXAS REFRIGERATOR ROLLS

1/2 cup sugar
2 tablespoons butter
2 cups boiling water
1-1/2 teaspoons salt
2 cakes compressed yeast
1/4 cup cold water
7 to 8 cups flour

Combine sugar, butter, boiling water, and salt. Cool, then add yeast dissolved in cold water. Add 4 cups flour, measured before sifting. Mix thoroughly. Add 3 to 4 more cups flour. Knead into firm dough as for bread. Store in refrigerator in covered greased bowl. Bake as needed. Makes 3 dozen.

VEGETABLES AND SIDE DISHES

Broccoli Casserole

1 (10-ounce) package frozen broccoli
1 (10-1/2-ounce) can cream of mushroom or chicken soup
2 eggs, beaten
1 cup mayonnaise
1-1/2 cups cheddar cheese, grated
crushed potato chips

Cook broccoli until tender; drain. Combine soup, eggs, mayonnaise, and cheese. Mix well. Add broccoli and pour into a buttered casserole dish; top with potato chips. Bake at 350° for 30 minutes or until brown and firm.

Baked Potatoes

4 russet potatoes, scrubbed
1 tablespoon solid vegetable shortening
butter
cheddar cheese, shredded
chopped chives
sour cream

Rub potatoes all over with shortening. Prick each potato several times with a fork. Bake at 350° for 1 hour and 15 minutes. Remove potatoes from oven and immediately cut a slit in the top of the potato to release steam. Serve with butter, cheese, chives, and sour cream. Makes 4 servings.

Spinach Casserole

1 small carton cottage cheese
1 cup cheddar cheese, grated
3 eggs
1/3 cup butter
3 tablespoons flour
1 package frozen chopped spinach, thawed
1/2 teaspoon salt

Combine all ingredients in a bowl and stir well. Pour into a greased casserole. Cover and bake at 350° for 30 to 45 minutes. Makes 6 to 8 servings.

Corn Casserole

1 large can corn
1 tablespoon onion, chopped
1 tablespoon pimento, minced
1 tablespoon bell pepper, chopped
1 (10-1/2-ounce) can cream of chicken soup
1 cup cooked rice
shredded cheese

In a saucepan, combine corn, onion, pimento, and bell pepper. Cook over medium heat until vegetables are tender, about 5 minutes. Mix in cream of chicken soup and cooked rice. Pour into a buttered casserole and cover with cheese. Bake at 350° for 20 minutes.

CORN PUDDING

1/2 cup milk
2 tablespoons butter, melted
1 teaspoon salt
2 tablespoons all-purpose flour
1 tablespoon soy sauce
2 cups canned cream-style corn
1 egg, well beaten
soft bread crumbs
1/4 cup fresh parsley, finely chopped

Combine milk, butter, salt, flour, soy sauce, corn, and egg in a mixing bowl and mix well. Pour the mixture into a casserole dish, sprinkle with bread crumbs, and bake at 350° for 30 minutes, or until firm. Sprinkle parsley over top just before serving.

POTATO AND CHEESE CASSEROLE

1 (2-pound) package frozen hash browns
1/2 cup butter, melted
1 teaspoon salt
1/2 teaspoon black pepper
1/2 cup onion, chopped
1 cup milk
1 (10-1/2-ounce) can cream of chicken soup
2 cups cheese, shredded
1 cup sour cream
2 cups potato chips, crushed

In a large casserole, mix the first five ingredients together. In a saucepan, combine milk, soup, cheese, and sour cream. Cook over medium heat until cheese melts. Pour over potatoes and onion in casserole. Top with potato chip crumbs. Bake at 350° for 1 hour. Let stand 10 to 15 minutes before serving.

Copper Penny Carrots

2 pounds carrots, sliced and cooked
1 medium onion, sliced
1 small green pepper, thinly sliced
1 can condensed tomato soup
1/2 cup oil
1 cup sugar
3/4 cup apple cider vinegar
salt
1 teaspoon mustard
1 teaspoon Worcestershire sauce

Arrange vegetables in a bowl. Mix together the rest of the ingredients in a saucepan. Bring to a boil and stir until well blended. Pour over vegetables. Refrigerate for about 2 hours.

Baked Beans

1 pound kidney beans
1 large onion, chopped
1/4 cup molasses
1/2 teaspoon dry mustard
1/3 cup brown sugar
3/4 teaspoon salt

Wash beans. Cover with water and boil 2 minutes. Let cool 1 hour. Drain and cover with fresh water. Boil until done but not mushy. Mix rest of ingredients in a slow cooker. Add beans and fresh water to cover. Turn slow cooker to high setting. Once it starts to boil, reduce heat to low, cover and cook for 6 to 8 hours.

GREEN BEAN CASSEROLE

3 (16-ounce) cans green beans, drained
3 slices bacon, cooked and crumbled
1 (10-1/2-ounce) can cream of mushroom soup
salt and pepper, to taste

Combine all ingredients in a casserole. Bake at 350° for 30 to 40 minutes.

CARROT CASSEROLE

2 cups carrots, cooked and mashed
1 cup brown sugar
3 tablespoons flour
1 teaspoon baking powder
1/2 cup butter, melted
3 eggs, beaten
1/4 teaspoon cinnamon

Combine all ingredients in order given. Bake at 400° for 15 minutes. Reduce heat to 350° and bake for 30 more minutes. Makes 6 to 8 servings.

BUTTER BEANS

1 slice bacon
1 (16-ounce) can butter beans, drained
1/8 teaspoon black pepper
1/8 teaspoon salt
1/8 teaspoon garlic powder

In a medium saucepan, cook bacon over medium heat. When bacon is brown, remove from saucepan and discard. Add beans and seasonings to saucepan and bring to a boil. Reduce heat and simmer for 10 minutes.

OKRA AND TOMATOES

1-1/2 pounds okra
1 tablespoon butter
1 onion, chopped
1 (16-ounce) can stewed tomatoes
1/2 teaspoon salt
1/4 teaspoon pepper

Wash okra, trim ends, and cut into 1/4-inch pieces. Sear okra in butter in a skillet. Add onion, tomatoes, salt, and pepper. Cook until tender, stirring constantly. Makes 6 servings.

VIDALIA ONION CASSEROLE

3 pounds Vidalia onions, thinly sliced
1/2 cup butter
1 cup rice, cooked
1-1/2 cups milk
8 ounces Swiss cheese, shredded
salt, to taste

Sauté onions in butter in a large skillet for 10 minutes or until tender. Add rice, milk, cheese, and salt; mix well. Spoon into a greased baking dish. Bake at 325° for 1 hour. Makes 6 servings.

SCALLOPED POTATOES

4 cups potatoes, thinly sliced
1 onion, thinly sliced
3 tablespoons flour
salt and pepper, to taste
3 tablespoons butter
1-1/4 cups milk, scalded

In a greased casserole, layer potatoes and onion alternately with flour, salt, and pepper. Dot with butter and pour scalded milk over top. Cover and bake at 350° for 1 hour or until brown.

CREAMED CORN

6 ears fresh corn, shucked
2 cups milk
2 tablespoons cornstarch
salt and pepper, to taste
2 tablespoons heavy cream
2 tablespoons butter

Lightly mash the corn kernels. In a saucepan, combine the corn, milk, and cornstarch. Cook over medium-high heat, stirring constantly, for 10 minutes. Remove from heat. Season with salt and pepper and add heavy cream and butter. Stir to combine.

EGGPLANT CASSEROLE

2 cups eggplant, cubed
2 tablespoons butter
1 cup mushrooms, sliced
1/3 cup onion, chopped
1/2 cup celery, chopped
1 egg, slightly beaten
1/3 cup milk
1/3 cup cheddar cheese, shredded
1 cup bread crumbs
grated Parmesan cheese

Steam eggplant until tender. In a skillet, melt 2 tablespoons butter and sauté the mushrooms. Add the onion and celery and sauté until tender. Add the eggplant and stir-fry briefly. Remove from heat. Beat together the egg, milk, cheese, and 1/2 cup bread crumbs. Pour into a buttered casserole. Top with remaining crumbs and Parmesan cheese. Cover and bake at 325° for 10 minutes. Remove cover and bake 15 more minutes.

SWEET POTATOES

5 medium sweet potatoes
1 teaspoon vanilla
1 teaspoon cinnamon
2 eggs, beaten
1 cup coconut
1 cup miniature marshmallows
1/2 cup pecans, chopped
1/4 cup brown sugar
1/8 cup butter

Boil sweet potatoes; drain and cream. Mix with vanilla, cinnamon, eggs, 3/4 cup coconut, 3/4 cup marshmallows, and pecans. Top with sugar and dot with butter. Sprinkle the remaining coconut and marshmallows on top. Bake at 350° for 20 to 30 minutes.

Squash Casserole

4 cups yellow squash, diced
2 cups zucchini, diced
1 teaspoon salt
1 onion, chopped
2 garlic cloves, finely chopped
1/4 cup butter
1/2 cup sour cream
1/2 teaspoon salt
1/2 teaspoon pepper
1 cup cheddar cheese, grated
1 cup saltine cracker crumbs

Put the squash and zucchini in a large saucepan. Add 1 teaspoon salt and cover with water; bring to a boil. Cook until the vegetables are soft, about 20 minutes.

In a skillet over medium-low heat, melt the butter. Add the onion and sauté until translucent, about 6 minutes. Add the garlic and cook until fragrant, about 1 minute. Remove from heat.

In a large bowl, combine squash, zucchini, onion, garlic, butter, sour cream, salt, pepper, and cheddar cheese. Mix well, then pour into a casserole. Top with cracker crumbs. Bake at 350° for 25 to 30 minutes.

Asparagus Casserole

2 cans asparagus
1 (10-1/2-ounce) can cream of mushroom soup
2 cups cracker crumbs
1 cup cheddar cheese, shredded

Layer asparagus, mushroom soup, and crackers in a greased casserole. Top with cheese and bake at 350° for 25 minutes.

Fried Green Tomatoes

1-1/2 cups flour
1/2 cup cornmeal
1 teaspoon sugar
2 teaspoons salt
1/4 teaspoon pepper
3/4 cup milk
4 green tomatoes, sliced
vegetable oil

Combine flour, cornmeal, sugar, salt, and pepper. Slowly add milk, stirring constantly, to form a batter. Dip tomato slices in batter and fry in hot oil. Drain on paper towels.

Tomato Casserole

6 slices bacon, chopped
1/2 cup onion, chopped
4 cups canned tomatoes
2 teaspoons brown sugar
1 teaspoon salt
1/2 teaspoon oregano
1/2 teaspoon pepper
4 slices bread
2 tablespoons butter
Parmesan cheese, grated

Fry bacon in a large skillet until partially cooked. Add onion and sauté until translucent. Stir in tomatoes, brown sugar, salt, oregano, and pepper. Tear bread into small pieces and add to the mixture. Pour into a buttered casserole dish. Dot with butter and sprinkle with Parmesan cheese. Bake at 350° for about 30 minutes or until bubbly. Makes 6 servings.

MASHED POTATOES

4 potatoes, peeled and cut into 1/2-inch pieces
1/2 cup milk
1/4 cup butter
salt and pepper, to taste

Cook potatoes in boiling water until tender, about 15 to 20 minutes. Drain water and mash potatoes. Stir in milk, butter, salt, and pepper.

POTATO CASSEROLE

1 (2-pound) package frozen southern style hash browns, thawed
1 (10-1/2-ounce) can cream of chicken soup
1/2 cup butter, melted
1/2 cup onion, chopped
1 pint sour cream
2 cups cheese, grated
1 teaspoon salt
1 teaspoon black pepper
cracker crumbs

Combine all ingredients except cracker crumbs and mix well. Pour into a lightly greased baking dish. Top with crushed cracker crumbs. Bake at 350° for 45 minutes.

TURNIP GREENS

4 strips bacon, sliced
1 onion, chopped
3 quarts water
1 teaspoon salt
1 teaspoon sugar
1 large bunch turnip greens, rinsed and patted dry

In a large pot, cook bacon until crispy. Add onion and sauté until tender. Add water, salt, and sugar; cover and bring to a boil. Add turnip greens and return to boil. Reduce heat and cook until greens are tender, about 1 to 2 hours.

COLLARD GREENS

2 ounces salt pork, sliced
3 Vidalia onions, finely chopped
8 garlic cloves, minced
1 large bunch collard greens, rinsed and patted dry
3 quarts chicken broth
1 teaspoon pepper
1 tablespoon seasoned salt
1/2 cup vinegar
4 teaspoons sugar

In a large pot, brown salt pork. Add onions and sauté until soft; add garlic and cook until fragrant, about 1 minute. Stir in collard greens, broth, pepper, seasoned salt, vinegar, and sugar. Bring to a boil; reduce heat and simmer, uncovered, until greens are tender, about 1 to 2 hours.

FRIED OKRA

1-1/2 cups buttermilk
1 egg
2 cups cornmeal
1-1/2 cups flour
1 teaspoon salt
1/2 teaspoon pepper
1 pound fresh okra, sliced into bite-sized pieces
vegetable oil, for frying

In a large bowl, mix together buttermilk and egg. In another bowl, combine cornmeal, flour, salt, and pepper. Soak okra in buttermilk mixture then dredge in cornmeal mixture. Fry in preheated oil until crispy. Drain.

BLACK-EYED PEAS

2 cups chicken broth
2 cups water
2 slices bacon
1 pound dried black-eyed peas, soaked overnight and drained
1 onion, chopped
1 jalapeño pepper, seeded and diced
salt and pepper, to taste

In a large pot, combine chicken broth, water, and bacon; bring to a boil. Reduce heat, cover, and simmer for 1 hour. Add peas to the pot along with onion, jalapeño pepper, salt, and pepper. Cover and cook until peas are tender, about 45 minutes.

BLACK BEANS AND RICE

2 large onions, chopped
3 green bell peppers, chopped
1 garlic clove, minced
1/2 cup olive oil
1 package black beans, soaked overnight and drained
1/2 ham bone or ham hock
8 cups water
3 bay leaves
1 tablespoon salt
1/4 cup vinegar (optional)
3 cups hot cooked rice
sour cream

In a stockpot, sauté onions, peppers, and garlic in the olive oil. Add the beans, ham bone, water, bay leaves, and salt. Bring to a boil and cook until beans are tender. Add vinegar and cook 5 minutes longer. Remove bay leaves. Serve beans over hot rice and garnish with chopped onion or sour cream. Makes 6 servings.

HOPPIN' JOHN

1 tablespoon olive oil
1 ham hock
1 onion, chopped
1/2 cup green bell pepper, chopped
2 garlic cloves, minced
1 pound dried black-eyed peas, soaked overnight and drained
6 cups chicken broth
1 bay leaf
2 sprigs fresh thyme
salt and pepper, to taste
3 cups rice, cooked

In a large pot, brown the ham hock in olive oil. Add onion, green bell pepper, and garlic; sauté 2 minutes. Add the black-eyed peas, chicken broth, bay leaf, thyme, salt, and pepper; bring to a boil. Reduce heat and simmer until peas are tender, about 45 minutes. Serve with rice.

GREEN BEANS

1-1/2 pounds green beans, trimmed
2 slices bacon, chopped
1 onion, chopped
2 garlic cloves, minced
salt and pepper, to taste

In a saucepan, cook green beans in boiling water for about 4 to 5 minutes. Drain. In a skillet, brown bacon over medium-high heat. Add onion and garlic to the skillet and cook until onion is tender. Add green beans to the skillet; stir well. Add salt and pepper.

BAKED EGGPLANT

3/4 cup seasoned bread crumbs
1/4 cup Parmesan cheese, grated
1/4 teaspoon salt
1/8 teaspoon pepper
1 large eggplant, cut into strips
1/2 cup olive oil

In a mixing bowl, combine bread crumbs, cheese, salt, and pepper. Toss eggplant strips in oil, then dip in breadcrumb mixture. Put coated strips on a foil-lined cookie sheet and bake at 375° for 15 to 20 minutes, or until golden.

STUFFED BELL PEPPERS

3 large bell peppers
1/2 pound ground chuck
1 cup bread crumbs
1 tablespoon onion, chopped
1 teaspoon salt
1/4 teaspoon pepper
1 can tomato sauce

Cut tops off peppers and hollow out inside. Wash peppers thoroughly and cook in salted boiling water. Mix remaining ingredients together and stuff inside peppers. Stand them upright in a baking dish and bake, covered, at 350° for 45 minutes. Remove the cover and cook for 15 more minutes.

STUFFED ARTICHOKES

4 medium artichokes
1 teaspoon salt
2/3 cup fine dry bread crumbs
1 garlic clove, peeled and sliced
1 teaspoon grated Parmesan cheese
1 teaspoon parsley, chopped
1 teaspoon salt
3/4 teaspoon pepper
2 garlic cloves, peeled and sliced
1 tablespoon parsley, chopped
2 cups boiling water
2 tablespoons olive oil

Cut off 1 inch from the top and base of each artichoke. Remove lower leaves. If desired, snip off tips of remaining leaves. Cover with cold water and add 1 teaspoon salt. Let stand 15 to 20 minutes. Drain upside-down.

Mix together bread crumbs, 1 clove sliced garlic, cheese, 1 teaspoon chopped parsley, salt, and pepper. Set aside.

Spread leaves of drained artichokes open slightly. Place 3 slices of garlic in each artichoke. Sprinkle with breadcrumb mixture between layers and over top of artichokes. Sprinkle with chopped parsley. Place artichokes close together in a skillet so they will remain upright during cooking. Pour the boiling water in the skillet and sprinkle the artichokes with olive oil. Cover and cook about 30 minutes, or until artichoke leaves are tender.

CHOW CHOW

3 cabbages
8 cups tomatoes
1 dozen onions
6 sweet bell peppers
6 red peppers
2 quarts vinegar
5 cups sugar
1 tablespoon salt

Chop all vegetables and toss together in a large pot. Add vinegar, sugar, and salt. Bring to boil and let boil for 30 minutes. Put into sterilized jars and seal.

CUCUMBER RELISH

12 large fresh cucumbers
8 green bell peppers
16 banana peppers
10 medium Vidalia onions
4 tablespoons plain salt
5 cups sugar
5-1/2 cups vinegar
3 tablespoons celery seed
6 tablespoons mustard seed

Slice cucumbers lengthwise and clean middle section. Grind cucumbers, peppers, and onions with coarse blade of grinder, or grate by hand. Add 4 tablespoons salt. Cover and refrigerate overnight. Drain through colander. Combine remaining ingredients. Mix all together and bring to a boil. Simmer 20 minutes. Pack in sterilized jars and seal.

SCALLOPED CORN

1 can cream style corn
1 can whole kernel corn
2 eggs, beaten
1/2 cup butter, melted
1 cup sour cream
1 box cornbread mix

Mix all ingredients together and bake in a pan at 375° for about 30 minutes.

SCALLOPED TOMATOES

2-1/2 cups bread crumbs
1/2 cup butter, melted
1 cup onions, chopped
2 tablespoons sugar
1 teaspoon salt
3-1/2 cups canned tomatoes, drained
1 cup cheddar cheese, grated

Toss bread crumbs with half of the butter and brown in a skillet. Remove bread crumbs and add onion to skillet. Cook until translucent, about 5 minutes. Add sugar, salt, and tomatoes. Pour into a buttered baking dish. Top with cheese and bread crumbs. Bake until cheese is melted and bread has browned, about 30 minutes.

CABBAGE CASSEROLE

6 cups cabbage, chopped
4 cups boiling water
1 teaspoon salt
2 tablespoons margarine
2 tablespoons flour
1/2 teaspoon salt
dash of pepper
3/4 cup sweet milk
3/4 cup cheddar cheese
1-1/4 cups buttered bread crumbs

Add cabbage and 1 teaspoon salt to boiling water . Cook 15 to 20 minutes uncovered; drain. Place cabbage in a greased casserole dish. Melt margarine, then add flour, salt, and pepper. Stir in milk and cook on low heat 5 minutes, stirring constantly. Remove from heat, blend in cheese, pour over cabbage. Top with crumbs. Bake at 350° for 20 minutes or until lightly browned.

CAULIFLOWER CASSEROLE

1 medium head cauliflower
2 pounds hamburger
1/2 cup bread crumbs
1 egg, slightly beaten
1 onion, minced
1 teaspoon salt
1/4 teaspoon pepper

Parboil cauliflower in salted water for 10 minutes. Drain thoroughly. Mix meat with crumbs, egg, onion, salt, and pepper. Cover bottom of deep baking dish with meat mixture. Place cauliflower on top and pour remaining meat mixture over that. Place dish in a pan of hot water and bake at 350° for 1 hour. Makes 8 servings.

Baked Carrots

4 cups cooked carrots, sliced
1-1/2 cups plain croutons
1 cup sharp cheddar cheese, grated
2 eggs, beaten
1/4 cup light cream or milk
1/4 cup margarine, melted
1-1/2 teaspoon Worcestershire sauce
1 teaspoon salt

Put carrots and croutons in a buttered casserole. Sprinkle with cheese. Mix together the rest of the ingredients and pour over. Bake, uncovered, at 400° for 20 minutes or until brown.

Southern Fried Squash

5 medium squash, peeled and sliced
1 onion, sliced
1 tablespoon bacon drippings
1/4 cup sugar
salt and pepper, to taste

Fry squash and onion in bacon drippings until heated through. Add sugar, salt, and pepper. Cover and steam until squash is tender. Remove cover. Cook until dry and lightly browned. Makes 6 servings.

STUFFED ZUCCHINI

6 medium zucchini squash
6 slices day-old bread, cubed
2 eggs
1 medium onion, finely chopped
salt and pepper, to taste
butter, melted
1/2 cup Parmesan cheese, grated

Wash zucchini well. Remove the stems and blossom ends; parboil for 7 minutes in salted water. Split lengthwise and scoop out the pulp. Pour cold water over cubed bread and squeeze dry. Chop the pulp of the squash and mix with the bread, eggs, onion, salt, and pepper. Stuff the squash shells with the pulp mixture. Drizzle butter over the tops and sprinkle with grated cheese. Arrange in a greased baking dish and bake at 350° for 30 minutes or until tender. Makes 6 servings.

CORNBREAD DRESSING

1/4 cup butter
1 cup onion, chopped
1/2 cup celery, chopped
3 cups chicken or turkey broth
6 cups cornbread, crumbled
3 cups torn white bread
2 to 3 eggs, beaten
2 teaspoons salt
1 teaspoon pepper

In a skillet, melt the butter and sauté the onion and celery. Stir in the broth and cook until tender. In a large bowl, combine the cornbread, white bread, eggs, salt, and pepper. Add the cooked onion and celery. Stir well to combine. Pour into a buttered casserole and bake at 450° for 30 minutes.

MACARONI AND CHEESE

2 tablespoons flour
1/4 teaspoon salt
3 tablespoons margarine, melted
2-1/2 cups milk
1 cup cheddar cheese, cubed
1/2 cup Swiss cheese, cubed
1/2 cup American cheese, cubed
1-1/2 cups elbow macaroni, cooked

Blend flour and salt into melted margarine in a large saucepan. Add milk all at once. Cook until thickened, stirring constantly. Stir in cheeses until melted. Fold in macaroni. Spoon into a greased baking dish. Bake at 350° for 25 minutes. Makes 8 servings.

DRESSING FROM THE HEARTLAND

1-1/2 cups onion, chopped
1-1/2 cups celery, diced
1-1/2 cups green pepper, diced
1/2 cup margarine
12 slices dried bread, cubed
1 teaspoon poultry seasoning
salt and pepper, to taste
1/4 teaspoon sage
1/2 cup turkey broth

In a medium-size skillet, over medium-high heat, sauté onion, celery, and green pepper in margarine until tender. In a large bowl combine onion mixture, bread cubes, poultry seasoning, salt, pepper, sage, and broth. Mix well. Spoon dressing into a lightly greased casserole. Cover and bake at 325° for 45 to 50 minutes. Uncover last 5 minutes of baking time.

This recipe used by permission of the National Turkey Federation.

MUSHROOM GRAVY

1 roasted turkey
3 tablespoons fat from poultry drippings
3 cups turkey broth
3 tablespoons all-purpose flour
1/2 teaspoon salt
1-1/2 tablespoons butter
1/2 pound button mushrooms, cleaned and sliced thin
salt and pepper, to taste

Remove the cooked turkey and roasting rack from the roasting pan. Pour poultry drippings through a sieve into a 4-cup measuring cup. Add 1 cup turkey broth to the roasting pan and stir until the crusty brown bits are loosened; pour the deglazed liquid/broth into the cup with drippings. Let the mixture stand a few minutes, until the fat rises to the top. Over medium heat, spoon 3 tablespoons fat from the poultry drippings into a saucepan. Whisk flour and salt into the heated fat and continue to cook and stir until the flour turns golden. Meanwhile, skim and discard any fat that remains on top of the poultry drippings. Add remaining broth to the poultry drippings.

Melt the butter in a large skillet over high heat. Add the mushrooms and sauté until the mushrooms are tender and all liquid has evaporated, about 3 to 4 minutes. Stir mushrooms into hot gravy. Season with salt and pepper. Cook and stir until gravy simmers and is slightly thick. Serve hot in a warm gravy boat.

This recipe used by permission of the National Turkey Federation.

DIRTY RICE

1 can onion soup
1 can chicken broth
1 cup uncooked rice
3/4 cup butter
pinch of salt

Combine all ingredients in a pan. Bake at 350° for 45 minutes.

RED BEANS AND RICE

2 tablespoons olive oil
2 pounds smoked sausage, sliced
1 green bell pepper, chopped
1 medium onion, chopped
2 to 3 tablespoons Creole seasoning
3 (15-1/2-ounce) cans red beans
1 (10-ounce) can diced tomatoes
salt and pepper, to taste
cooked rice

Heat olive oil in a large skillet over medium-high heat. Add sausage and next 3 ingredients. Cook, stirring frequently, until sausage is brown and vegetables are tender. Add red beans and tomatoes, stirring well. Season with salt and pepper. Reduce heat to low and simmer, stirring occasionally, about 30 minutes. Serve over hot rice.

RICE CASSEROLE

1 cup rice, uncooked
1 can beef consomme
1 can French onion soup
1 can mushrooms, including liquid
1/2 cup butter

Combine all ingredients in a casserole. Bake at 325° for 1-1/2 hours or until all liquid is gone. Makes 6 to 8 servings.

MACARONI CASSEROLE

1 (14-ounce) package macaroni and cheese
1 (10-1/2-ounce) can cream of mushroom soup, undiluted
1 (4-ounce) jar diced pimento, drained
1/4 cup green bell pepper, diced
1/2 cup milk
1/4 cup onion, chopped
1/3 cup mayonnaise
1 cup cheese, grated

Cook macaroni according to package directions; drain well. Add the pouch of cheese sauce from the packages well as the mushroom soup, pimento, green bell pepper, milk, onion, and mayonnaise; mix well. Spoon into a well-greased casserole. Bake, uncovered, at 400° for 20 minutes. Sprinkle cheese on top and bake 5 minutes more. Makes 6 servings.

GLAZED CARROTS

2 pounds carrots, peeled and sliced
1/2 cup water
3 tablespoons brown sugar
3 tablespoons honey
2 tablespoons margarine

Bring carrots to a boil in water in a saucepan; reduce heat. Cover and simmer for 8 minutes. Add brown sugar, honey, and margarine; mix gently. Simmer over low heat until carrots are glazed. Makes 8 servings.

BEEF AND PORK

Pot Roast

1 (4-pound) boneless chuck roast
1/2 teaspoon salt
1/2 teaspoon pepper
1/2 teaspoon garlic powder
1/4 cup vegetable oil
1 cup onion, chopped
1 cup carrot, chopped
1 cup celery, chopped
2 garlic cloves, minced
3 bay leaves
4 cups beef broth
1/2 cup apple cider
4 tablespoons butter
4 tablespoons flour

Season roast with salt, pepper, and garlic powder. In a large roasting pan, sear roast over high heat in oil. Remove roast from pan and reduce heat to medium. Add onion, carrot, celery, and garlic and cook in meat drippings until tender. Return the roast to the pan and add bay leaves, beef broth, and apple cider; bring to a simmer. Skim the surface and cover tightly. Bake at 350° for 2-1/2 to 3 hours. Turn the roast over periodically.

When the roast is done, remove pan from oven and transfer roast to a cutting board. Cover with aluminum foil. Skim the liquid in the pan and bring to a boil. Slowly stir in the butter and flour, in equal parts, a little bit at a time until the sauce is of desired consistency. Pour sauce over roast and serve.

POTATO AND BEEF CASSEROLE

1 pound ground round
1/2 onion, finely chopped
1-1/2 cups mild cheddar cheese, shredded
salt and pepper, to taste
4 potatoes, thinly sliced
1 (10-1/2-ounce) can cream of mushroom soup
1/2 cup milk

Brown ground round and onion in a skillet, stirring until ground round is crumbly; drain. Spread beef mixture in baking dish; sprinkle with cheese, salt, and pepper. Layer potatoes over cheese. Spread mixture of soup and milk over top. Bake at 350° for 90 minutes. Makes 6 servings.

GROUND BEEF AND NOODLE BAKE

2 tablespoons butter
2 pounds ground beef
2 (8-ounce) cans tomato sauce
1 teaspoon sugar
1 teaspoon salt
pepper, to taste
1 (8-ounce) package noodles, cooked and drained
1 (8-ounce) package cream cheese, chopped
1 cup sour cream
3 green onions, chopped
1/2 cup mild cheddar cheese, shredded

Melt butter in skillet and add beef. Stir until crumbly; drain. Add
tomato sauce, sugar, salt, and pepper; mix well. Simmer, covered, for
15 minutes. Layer noodles, cream cheese, sour cream, green onions,
and ground beef mixture 1/2 at a time in a greased large baking dish.
Top with cheese. Bake at 350° for 30 to 45 minutes or until heated
through. Makes 8 servings.

CORNED BEEF CASSEROLE

1 package noodles
1 cup onion, chopped
1 cup bell pepper, chopped
1/3 cup butter
1 (10-1/2-ounce) can cream of mushroom soup
1 (10-1/2-ounce) can cream of celery soup
1 can corned beef
1 cup milk
1 (4-ounce) jar sliced mushrooms
1 cup grated cheese

Cook noodles. Sauté onion and pepper in butter. Add soups, corned beef, and milk. In a greased baking pan, layer noodles and sauce. Garnish with mushrooms and cheese. Bake at 350° for 1 hour.

MEATLOAF

2 eggs, beaten
1/3 cup milk
1/2 cup tomato sauce
1 teaspoon salt
dash of pepper
1-1/2 cups bread crumbs
2 pounds ground beef
1 cup onion, finely chopped
1 green bell pepper, chopped
1 cup tomatoes, diced
1/4 tablespoon Worcestershire sauce

Combine eggs, milk, and tomato sauce in a large bowl. Add salt and pepper; stir to combine. Add bread crumbs, ground beef, onion, green bell pepper, tomatoes, and Worcestershire sauce. Place mixture into a loaf pan and bake at 375° for 45 minutes to 1 hour.

Texas Hash

1-1/2 pounds ground beef
2 cups onion, chopped
2 cups bell pepper, chopped
1 tablespoon chili powder
1 tablespoon salt
1/2 teaspoon pepper
1/2 teaspoon garlic powder
2 cups canned tomatoes
3 cups cooked rice

Sauté beef, onion, pepper, and seasonings until meat is no longer pink and vegetables are tender. Add tomatoes and rice. Spoon into a casserole. Bake at 350° for 25 minutes.

Rice and Hamburger Casserole

1 pound ground beef
1 onion, chopped
celery, diced
1 tablespoon margarine
salt and pepper, to taste
1/8 cup soy sauce
1 (10-1/2-ounce) can cream of mushroom soup
1 (10-1/2-ounce) can cream of chicken soup
2 cups cooked rice

In a large skillet, brown the beef. In a saucepan, sauté the onion and celery in the margarine. Combine the browned beef, sautéed onion and celery, and the rest of the ingredients in a casserole dish. Bake at 325° for 1 hour. Makes 6 servings.

BEEF BRISKET

2 tablespoons Worcestershire sauce
2 tablespoons liquid smoke
1 teaspoon garlic salt
1-1/2 teaspoons salt
2 teaspoons pepper
3 to 4 pounds beef brisket

Rub sauce and seasoning on all sides of meat. Turn fat side up and let marinate over night. Cover and cook at 300° for 5 to 6 hours. Pour off meat drippings and refrigerate until fat hardens (remove and discard). Heat meat drippings; pour over thinly sliced brisket.

SLOPPY JOES

1-1/2 pounds ground beef
2/3 cup onion, chopped
1/2 cup celery, diced
1/4 cup green bell pepper, diced
1 tablespoon Worcestershire sauce
1/2 teaspoon salt
1/8 teaspoon pepper
1/2 cup ketchup
hamburger buns

In a large saucepan, cook beef, onion, celery, and green pepper over medium-high heat, until beef is browned. Drain. Add Worcestershire sauce, salt, pepper, and ketchup. Stir to combine, reduce heat to medium, and cook for 5 more minutes. Spoon on buns.

COUNTRY-FRIED STEAK

1/2 teaspoon salt
1/2 teaspoon pepper
1-1/2 cups flour
2 pounds boneless round steak
1 cup vegetable oil
1 onion, chopped
3 cups water

Combine salt, pepper, and flour in a large bowl. Dredge steaks in flour mixture. Reserve any flour left over. Heat oil in a large skillet over medium-high heat. Brown steaks on both sides. Remove steaks from the skillet and reduce heat. Add onion and sauté until tender. Combine remaining flour and water; blend well. Pour flour mixture into the skillet and stir slowly until it begins to thicken. Return steaks to skillet. Let simmer, covered, for 15 minutes or until steaks are cooked through.

PEPPER STEAK

2 pounds round steak, cut into 1/2-inch strips
salt
1/4 teaspoon pepper
1/4 cup flour
1/4 cup cooking oil
1 (1-pound) can tomatoes
1-3/4 cups beef stock
1/2 cup onion, chopped
1 garlic clove, minced
2 large green bell peppers, cut into strips
1-1/2 teaspoons Worcestershire sauce

Season the steak with salt. Mix 1/2 teaspoon salt and pepper with 1/4 cup flour. Dredge meat and brown in hot oil. Set aside remaining seasoned flour. Drain tomatoes, reserving liquid. Add tomato liquid, beef stock, onion, and garlic to the meat in the skillet. Cover and simmer for 1-1/4 hours. Add green pepper strips and Worcestershire sauce, and simmer for 5 minutes more. Finally, blend in tomatoes and reserved flour and simmer about 5 minutes. Makes 6 servings.

HAMBURGER STEAKS WITH ONION GRAVY

1 pound ground beef
1 egg
1/2 cup oatmeal
1/2 teaspoon garlic salt
2/3 cup tomato juice
2 cups onion, sliced
1/4 cup flour
2 cups beef stock

Mix first five ingredients and make into medium-sized steaks; brown in a skillet and put into a casserole. Brown the onion in the skillet; add flour and mix well. Let brown. Pour in the beef stock and cook until smooth. Pour over steaks and cook at 400° for 20 minutes.

MEATBALLS

3 pounds ground beef
2 cups oatmeal
1 (12-ounce) can evaporated milk
1 cup onion, chopped
1 egg
2 teaspoons chili powder
1/2 teaspoon garlic powder
2 teaspoons salt
1/2 teaspoon pepper
tomato sauce

Combine all ingredients except tomato sauce and mix well. Spoon onto a greased baking pan. Pour tomato sauce over top and bake at 350° for 1 hour.

SCALLOPED LIVER AND POTATOES

6 potatoes
1 pound liver
1 onion, minced
1 green bell pepper, chopped
1-1/4 teaspoons salt
1-1/2 cups milk

Boil the potatoes in their jackets; when done, peel and cut in slices. Drop the liver in boiling salted water and cook from 5 to 10 minutes. Cut into small pieces. Grease a baking dish. Cover the bottom with a layer of potatoes, add a layer of liver, and sprinkle with onions, green peppers, and seasoning. Repeat until the ingredients are used. Add milk and bake at 350° for 30 minutes .

BARBECUE SHORT RIBS

8 lean short ribs
2 tablespoons Worcestershire sauce
2 tablespoons brown sugar
3 tablespoons vinegar
6 tablespoons onion, chopped
1 tablespoon ketchup
1/2 cup water

Brown short ribs on all sides. Place in a casserole. Mix together the rest of the ingredients and pour over ribs. Cover and bake at 325° for 1-1/2 hours.

HAM CASSEROLE

1 (10-1/2-ounce) can cream of mushroom soup, undiluted
1/2 cup milk
1 teaspoon onion, minced
2 teaspoons mustard
1 cup sour cream
4 ounces noodles, cooked
2 cups leftover cooked ham, cut in 1-inch pieces
1/4 cup dry bread crumbs
1-1/2 tablespoons butter, melted
1 tablespoon Parmesan cheese, grated

In a saucepan, combine soup and milk, stirring until smooth. Add onion, mustard, and sour cream, stirring to combine well. In prepared casserole, layer half of the noodles, ham, and sauce. Repeat. Toss bread crumbs with butter; sprinkle over casserole. Top with cheese. Bake at 350°, uncovered, for 25 to 30 minutes or until golden brown.

HAM LOAF

3/4 pound ground beef
3/4 pound cooked ham
1 cup uncooked rolled oats
1 cup bread crumbs
1/4 cup onions, minced
1/4 cup green bell pepper, chopped
1/4 cup ketchup
1 teaspoon salt
1/4 teaspoon pepper
1 (10-1/2-ounce) cream of mushroom or cream of celery soup
1 can of water

Combine ingredients in a large bowl. Mix well. Pack into a greased pan. Chill. Bake at 350° for 1 hour and 15 minutes. Serves 8.

Pork Chops

8 center-cut or butterflied pork chops
salt and pepper, to taste
1/2 cup flour
2 tablespoons oil
1 cup sour cream
1 (10-1/2-ounce) can cream of mushroom soup
1 package onion soup mix
1 cup apple cider

Rinse pork chops and pat dry. Sprinkle with salt and pepper; coat
with flour. Brown on both sides in oil in skillet; drain well. Arrange in
a single layer in a rectangular baking dish. Combine sour cream,
soup, soup mix, and apple cider in a bowl; mix well. Spoon over pork
chops. Bake at 325° for 45 minutes. Makes 8 servings.

Pork Chop Casserole

6 medium potatoes, sliced
2 medium onions, sliced
2 large carrots, sliced
1 (10-1/2-ounce) can cream of mushroom soup
1/2 cup milk
6 pork chops
salt and pepper, to taste

Place potatoes in a buttered casserole, then onions and carrots. Mix
soup and milk. Pour over vegetables. Season pork chops with salt and
pepper and place on top of vegetables. Bake at 400°, uncovered, until
slightly brown. Turn pork chops over once. Cover with foil and bake
about 1-1/2 hours. Makes 6 servings.

Pork Chops with Milk Gravy

3 tablespoons flour
1 teaspoon salt
1/8 teaspoon pepper
4 pork chops, about 1 pound
1/2 tablespoon oil
1 cup water
1/2 cup evaporated milk

Combine the flour, salt, and pepper. Roll the pork chops in the flour mixture. Sprinkle over chops any flour that is left. Brown the chops on both sides in hot oil. Add water, cover, and cook slowly 30 minutes, or until tender. Remove chops to warm platter. Stir evaporated milk into skillet, heat until steaming hot, but do not boil. Pour over chops.

Hillbilly Sausage and Sweet Potatoes

2 pounds sweet potatoes
1/2 cup sugar
1/2 cup brown sugar
2 tablespoons butter
1 teaspoon salt
1/4 cup water
1 pound sausage links

Parboil potatoes 15 minutes; peel and cut into strips. Put in a well-greased baking pan. Mix sugars, butter, salt, and water thoroughly. Bring to a boil in a saucepan and cook for 3 minutes. Pour over the potatoes and bake 40 minutes at 350°. Put sausage on top and bake another 30 minutes.

Pork Roast

1 (2-pound) pork roast
1 cup water
1 to 2 teaspoons rosemary, chopped
5 potatoes, peeled and cut in half
2 carrots, peeled and cut in half

Place roast in a slow cooker; add water and rosemary. Cover and cook on low for 3 hours. Add vegetables and cook for 2 hours longer.

Baked Pork Tenderloin

1 (1-1/2-pound) pork tenderloin, sliced to 1-inch pieces
garlic powder
thyme
1 (10-1/2-ounce) can golden mushroom soup
1/4 cup apple cider

Place pork slices in a shallow baking dish. Sprinkle garlic powder and thyme on top. Combine the soup and the apple cider, then pour over pork. Bake, uncovered, at 325° for about 45 minutes, or until bubbly. Makes 4 servings.

Sausage Jambalaya

1 pound hot sausage
1 cup red and green bell pepper, chopped
1 cup celery, diced
1 cup sweet onion, chopped
1 cup cooked rice
1-1/2 cups tomatoes, diced
salt and pepper, to taste

Cook sausage and drain well. Sauté pepper, celery, and onion in 1 tablespoon sausage drippings until tender. Add rice, tomatoes, salt, and pepper; cook until heated through, about 30 minutes. Makes 4 servings.

POULTRY

OVEN-FRIED CHICKEN

6 to 8 pieces chicken
1/2 cup flour
1 teaspoon salt
1/4 teaspoon pepper
1/2 teaspoon paprika
1/2 cup margarine, melted

Rinse chicken and pat dry. Coat with mixture of flour, salt, pepper, and paprika. Pour melted margarine in a baking pan. Dip chicken pieces in margarine; arrange in pan. Bake at 400° for 30 minutes; turn. Bake for 25 minutes, or until chicken is tender. Makes 8 servings.

SOUTHERN FRIED CHICKEN

1 (3 to 4-pound) chicken, cut into pieces
1 teaspoon salt
1 teaspoon pepper
2 cups buttermilk
2 cups flour
1 teaspoon garlic powder
1 teaspoon paprika
vegetable oil, for frying

Season chicken with salt and pepper. In a large dish, pour buttermilk over chicken. Allow to soak for 2 hours. Combine flour, garlic powder, and paprika. Dredge chicken in flour mixture and fry, a few pieces at a time, in preheated oil until golden brown, 8 to 10 minutes for white meat and 12 to 14 minutes for dark meat. Remove from oil and drain.

CHICKEN CASSEROLE

1 (3-pound) chicken, cut up
salt and pepper, to taste
6 slices bacon
2 cups rice, uncooked
1 (10-ounce) can cream of mushroom soup
2 cups milk

Rinse chicken and pat dry. Season with salt and pepper. Arrange bacon in baking dish. Sprinkle rice over bacon. Arrange chicken over rice. Pour mixture of soup and milk over top. Bake at 350° for 90 minutes. Makes 6 servings.

CHICKEN AND DUMPLINGS

1 (3-pound) chicken
1 (10-ounce) can cream of chicken soup
4 cups flour
1/2 cup shortening
1 cup cold water
1 teaspoon salt

Rinse chicken and pat dry. Combine chicken and enough water to cover in a stockpot. Cook until tender. Remove to platter, reserving broth. Chop chicken, discarding skin and bones. Stir soup into chicken broth. Combine flour, shortening, water, and salt in a bowl; mix well. Knead just until stiff dough forms. Roll thin on lightly floured surface; cut into 1/2-inch strips. Drop into chicken broth mixture. Cook over low heat until tender. Stir in chicken. Makes 8 servings.

CHICKEN POT PIE

2 cups chicken, cooked and chopped
1 large onion, chopped
1/2 cup carrots, chopped
1/2 cup English peas
1 (10-1/2-ounce) can mushroom soup
salt and pepper, to taste
3 cups chicken broth
2 (9-inch) pie shells, unbaked

Combine chicken, onion, carrots, peas, soup, salt, pepper, and chicken broth. Pour into one of the pie shells. Top with remaining pie shell and crimp edges to seal. Cut vents in the top. Bake at 350° for 45 minutes.

ROASTED CHICKEN

1 (3 to 4-pound) chicken
3 tablespoons butter
3 garlic cloves, minced
1 teaspoon salt
1 tablespoon pepper
3 sprigs rosemary
3 sprigs thyme
1 lemon, quartered

Rub the entire chicken with a mixture of butter, garlic, salt, and pepper. Place the rosemary and thyme sprigs, along with the lemon, inside the lower cavity. Tie legs together with butcher's string if necessary. Place on a lightly greased roasting pan and bake at 450° for 30 minutes. Reduce heat to 350° and bake for 1 hour, or until done.

CHEESE AND CHICKEN ROLL UPS

1/4 cup butter
1/3 cup flour
5 cups chicken broth
4 cups ground chicken
1 tablespoon onion, finely chopped
1/4 cup pimento, chopped
salt and pepper
1 can biscuit dough
1/2 cup processed cheese spread

In a large saucepan, melt the butter. Add flour and 3 cups chicken broth; stir until thickened. Add chicken, onion, and pimento. Season with salt and pepper and cook until chicken is browned.

Spread biscuit dough out onto a floured surface. Spread evenly with cheese spread then add chicken mixture. Roll up like a jelly roll, seal edge, and cut into 12 slices. Place 1 inch apart on a greased baking sheet. Bake at 375° for about 30 minutes.

LEMON PEPPER CHICKEN

1-1/4 pounds chicken breast fillets
1 cup bread crumbs
2 tablespoons parsley, chopped
1 tablespoon lemon rind, grated
1 teaspoon pepper
1/2 teaspoon salt
1/4 cup plain yogurt

Rinse chicken fillets and pat dry. Combine bread crumbs with parsley, grated lemon rind, pepper, and salt. Brush fillets with yogurt then coat with bread crumbs. Place on a nonstick baking sheet. Bake at 375° for 20 minutes or until tender. Makes 5 servings.

SOUTHERN BAKED CHICKEN

1 teaspoon chili powder
1 teaspoon paprika
1/4 teaspoon garlic powder
1/4 teaspoon salt
1/4 teaspoon pepper
2/3 cup self-rising cornmeal
1 (2-1/2 to 3-pound) chicken, cut into pieces
1/4 cup milk
1/4 cup butter, melted

Combine the chili powder, paprika, garlic powder, salt, pepper, and cornmeal. Dip pieces of chicken in the milk and dredge in cornmeal mixture. Place chicken, skin side up, on a greased baking dish. Lightly brush with melted butter. Bake at 375° for 50 to 55 minutes, or until juices run clear when chicken is pierced by a fork. Makes 4 servings.

SUNDAY CHICKEN

1 (10-1/2-ounce) can cream of mushroom soup
1 (10-1/2-ounce) can cream of celery soup
1 (10-1/2-ounce) can cream of chicken soup
1/3 cup melted butter, divided
1-1/4 cup quick cooking rice
1 (3 to 4-pound) chicken, cut into pieces
salt and pepper, to taste
paprika

In a medium bowl, combine soups, 1/4 of the butter, and the rice. Pour into a greased dish. Place chicken pieces over rice mixture and brush with remaining butter. Season with salt and pepper. Sprinkle with paprika. Bake at 275° about 2-1/2 hours, or until tender. Makes 4 to 6 servings.

CREAMED CHICKEN

3 tablespoons butter
4 tablespoons flour
1 cup chicken stock
1 cup milk
2 cups cooked chicken, chopped
3 hard-boiled eggs, peeled and chopped
1/2 teaspoon salt
1/2 teaspoon pepper

Melt butter; add flour and stir over low heat until well blended. Add chicken stock and milk. Cook over low heat until thickened and smooth. Add chopped chicken and eggs; season with salt and pepper. Serve over hot biscuits.

CHICKEN AND YELLOW RICE

2 pounds chicken pieces: thighs, breasts, and legs
3 tablespoons olive oil
1 green bell pepper, chopped
1 onion, chopped
1 garlic clove, chopped
4 tomatoes, chopped
1 pint water
1 bay leaf
1 pound rice
dash of saffron

Brown chicken in olive oil in a large pot. Remove chicken and cover to keep warm. Add bell pepper, onion, garlic, tomatoes, rice, water, and bay leaf to the pot. Bring to a boil, then add chicken, rice, and saffron. Cover and cook until rice is done, about 20 to 25 minutes.

TURKEY CASSEROLE

4 ounces margarine, divided
4 ounces onions, diced
4 ounces celery, diced
3-1/2 quarts cooked noodles, rinsed and drained
8 cups turkey gravy
2-1/2 pounds cooked turkey, diced
1/4 cup red bell pepper, diced
4 ounces fine, dry bread crumbs

Heat 2 ounces margarine and sauté onions and celery until just tender. Add noodles, gravy, turkey, and peppers. Blend well.

Pour into a casserole. Melt remaining 2 ounces margarine. Combine with bread crumbs. Sprinkle crumb mixture on top of casserole. Bake at 350° until the casserole reaches 160°.

This recipe used by permission of the National Turkey Federation.

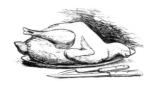

NORTH CAROLINA BARBECUE TURKEY

1 (10 to 12-pound) whole turkey, fresh or thawed
cooking oil
1-1/2 pounds turkey bacon
salt and pepper, to taste
1 tablespoon red pepper flakes, crushed
2 cups apple cider vinegar
1 cup cold water

Cut turkey in half, rub with oil, and wrap with bacon. (If turkey is more than 12 pounds, use bacon substitute, as real bacon will burn.) Prepare grill for medium indirect heat cooking. For gas grills, place a drip pan under one half of the rack then spray the rack with nonstick cooking spray, and turn on the heat on the other half of the grill. For charcoal grills, place the coals around the outside edges of the grill, place a drip pan in the center, spray the rack, and light the charcoal. Place turkey, breast side up, on grill rack over drip pan. Cover and grill turkey 2-1/2 to 3 hours or until meat thermometer inserted into deepest portion of thigh reaches 180° and leg bone will turn and separate from meat. Turkey should be golden brown.

Allow turkey to cool. Remove turkey from bones and chop. Add salt and pepper to taste. Sprinkle with red pepper flakes and mix well. Mix vinegar and water and sprinkle over meat. Stir gently into chopped turkey. Add water if vinegar mixture is too strong.

This recipe used by permission of the National Turkey Federation.

HOT BROWN SANDWICH

1/2 cup unsalted butter
1/3 cup flour
3 to 3-1/2 cups milk
1/3 cup Parmesan cheese, grated
1 large egg, beaten
1 tablespoon whipping cream
salt and freshly ground black pepper, to taste
10 slices white bread, toasted
1 pound oven roasted turkey breast, sliced thin
Parmesan cheese, grated
10 slices turkey bacon, cooked
10 slices red ripe tomatoes

Melt butter and stir in flour to make a reasonably thick roux, stirring until smooth and light brown. Stir in milk gradually and whisk to blend. Blend in Parmesan cheese. Continue to cook until thickened, stirring constantly. Beat a little of the hot mixture with the egg. Remove sauce from heat and beat in the egg mixture. Fold in cream. Add salt and pepper to taste.

For each Hot Brown sandwich, place two slices of toast on a flameproof dish. Cover the toast with 3 ounces of cooked turkey. Pour a generous amount of sauce over the turkey. Sprinkle with additional Parmesan cheese. Place entire dish under a broiler and broil until the sauce is speckled brown and bubbly. Remove from broiler, cross two pieces of cooked bacon on top, and serve immediately. Garnish with tomato slices, if desired.

This recipe used by permission of the National Turkey Federation.

PECAN CRUSTED TURKEY TENDERLOINS

1-1/2 cups dry bread crumbs
1-1/2 cups pecans, very finely chopped
1 teaspoon fresh parsley, chopped
1/4 teaspoon poultry seasoning
1/4 teaspoon fine black pepper
2 eggs
1 cup water
**1 to 1-1/2 pounds turkey tenderloins, pounded to an even
  thickness**

Mix first five ingredients together in a shallow dish. Mix eggs and water together in another shallow dish. Dip turkey tenderloins into egg wash and roll in dry mixture. Spray a baking pan with non-stick cooking spray. Place turkey in prepared pan. Bake at 350° until no longer pink in the center and the internal temperature reaches 170°, about 30 minutes.

This recipe used by permission of the National Turkey Federation.

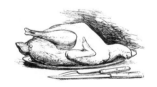

Southern Roasted Turkey with Peach Glaze

1 (15-pound) whole turkey, thawed if frozen
1-1/2 teaspoons salt
1/2 teaspoon freshly ground black pepper
1 medium orange, cut in wedges
1/2 cup peach preserves
2 tablespoons water
2 teaspoons orange juice
pickled peaches, for garnish

Remove giblets and neck from turkey; reserve for gravy. Blot turkey dry with clean paper towels. Sprinkle salt and pepper in the cavities of the bird. Insert orange wedges into both cavities. Fold neck skin and fasten to the back with skewers. Fold the wings under the back of the turkey. Return legs to tucked position.

Place turkey, breast side up, on a rack in a large shallow (no more than 2-1/2-inches deep) roasting pan. Insert an oven-safe thermometer into thickest part of the thigh, being careful it does not touch the bone. Roast turkey at 325° about 3-3/4 hours. Baste with the pan juices.

Meanwhile, in a small saucepan, over low heat, combine preserves, water, and orange juice. Cook until preserves are melted. During the last 30 minutes of roasting time, baste the bird with the peach glaze. Continue to roast until the thermometer registers 180° in the thigh and 170° in the breast. Remove turkey from the oven, remove the orange wedges, and allow the bird to rest for 15 to 20 minutes before carving. Place on a warm platter and garnish with pickled peaches.

This recipe used by permission of the National Turkey Federation.

GIBLET GRAVY

1 package neck, heart, gizzard from turkey giblets
1 medium carrot, thickly sliced
1 medium onion, thickly sliced
1 medium celery rib, thickly sliced
1/2 teaspoon salt
1 turkey liver
3 tablespoons fat from turkey drippings
3 tablespoons all-purpose flour
1/2 teaspoon salt
pepper, to taste

In a saucepan, over high heat, place neck, heart, gizzard, vegetables, and 1/2 teaspoon salt in enough cold water to cover. Heat to boiling. Reduce heat to low; cover and simmer 45 minutes. Add liver and simmer 15 minutes longer. Strain broth into a large bowl; cover and reserve broth in the refrigerator.

To make gravy, remove cooked turkey and roasting rack from the roasting pan. Strain poultry drippings through a sieve into a 4-cup measuring cup. Add 1 cup giblet broth to the roasting pan and stir until the crusty brown bits are loosened; pour the deglazed liquid/broth into cup with drippings. Let the mixture stand a few minutes, until the fat rises to the top. Over medium heat, spoon 3 tablespoons fat from the poultry drippings into a 2-quart saucepan. Whisk flour and 1/2 teaspoon salt into the heated fat and continue to cook and stir until the flour turns golden.

Meanwhile, skim and discard any fat remaining on top of the poultry drippings. Add remaining broth and enough water to the poultry drippings to equal 3-1/2 cups. Gradually whisk in warm poultry drippings/broth mixture. Cook and stir until gravy simmers and is slightly thick. Season to taste.

This recipe used by permission of the National Turkey Federation.

Southern Deep Fried Turkey

1 (10 to 12-pound) whole turkey, non self-basting
1 cup vinaigrette
2 teaspoons lemon pepper seasoning salt
1 teaspoon garlic powder
1 teaspoon onion powder
1 teaspoon cayenne pepper
peanut oil

Remove the giblets and neck, rinse the turkey well with cold water and pat dry thoroughly with paper towels. Take care to dry both inside cavities. To allow for good oil circulation throughout the cavity, do not truss or tie legs together. Cut off the wing tips and plump little tail as they may get caught in the fryer basket.

In a medium bowl, mix vinaigrette and seasonings together. Strain the marinade. Place the marinade in an injection syringe. Inject the marinade in the turkey breast, thighs, and legs. Place the bird in a large plastic bag, refrigerate, and marinate for at least 2 hours. Turn the bag and massage the turkey from time to time. Drain the turkey from the marinade and discard marinade. Place the turkey in the fryer basket or on a rack, neck down.

Place the outdoor gas burner on a level dirt or grassy area. Never fry a turkey indoors, in a garage, or in any structure attached to a building. Do not fry on wood decks, which could catch fire, or concrete, which could be stained by the oil. Have a fire extinguisher nearby for added safety.

Add oil to a 7 to 10 gallon pot with a basket or rack. At the medium-high setting, heat the oil to 375° (depending on the amount of oil, outside temperature, and wind conditions, this should take about 40 minutes). Slowly lower the turkey into the hot oil. The level of the oil will rise due to the frothing caused by the moisture from the turkey but will stabilize in about one minute. To prevent burns from the splattering oil, wear oven mitts/gloves, long sleeves, heavy shoes, and even glasses. It is wise to have two people lowering and raising the turkey.

Immediately check the oil temperature and increase the flame so the oil temperature is maintained at 350°. If the temperature drops to 340° or below, oil will begin to seep into the turkey.

Fry about 3 to 4 minutes per pound, or about 35 to 42 minutes for a 10 to 12-pound turkey. Stay with the cooker at all times, as the heat must be regulated. When cooked to 170° in the breast or 180° in the thigh, carefully remove the turkey from the hot oil. Allow the turkey to drain for a few minutes. Allow the oil to cool completely before storing or disposing. Remove turkey from the rack and place on a serving platter. Allow to rest for 20 minutes before carving.

Note: Use only oils with high smoke points, such as peanut, canola, or safflower oil. To determine the correct amount of oil, place the turkey in the pot before adding seasoning and add water until turkey is covered. Measure the amount of water and use a corresponding amount of oil. Dry the pot thoroughly of all water.

This recipe used by permission of the National Turkey Federation.

CAROLINA MINCED TURKEY BARBECUE

2 cups grilled turkey
1/2 cup cider vinegar
1/2 cup water
2 tablespoons molasses
1/2 to 3/4 teaspoon red pepper flakes
1/2 teaspoon black pepper
1/2 teaspoon salt
4 sandwich buns, split horizontally and toasted
1-1/2 cups deli coleslaw

Cut meat from bones and mince. In a saucepan, over high heat, combine vinegar, water, molasses, red pepper flakes, black pepper, and salt with minced turkey. Bring mixture to boil, reduce heat, cover and simmer 30 minutes. Uncover and simmer additional 30 to 35 minutes or until liquid has evaporated. To serve, spoon barbecue mixture over burger buns and top with coleslaw.

This recipe used by permission of the National Turkey Federation.

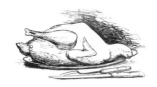

HOME-STYLE TURKEY POT PIE

1 tablespoon butter
1 small sweet onion, chopped
1/2 cup carrots, peeled and chopped
1/2 cup potatoes, peeled and chopped
1/2 cup celery, chopped
1/2 teaspoon salt
1/2 teaspoon dried thyme
1/2 teaspoon dried rosemary, crushed
pinch black pepper
1 bay leaf
2 cups turkey broth
1/3 cup flour
1 cup frozen peas
2 cups cooked turkey, chopped
2 (9-inch) pie shells
2 tablespoons milk

In a saucepan, melt butter over medium heat. Add onion, carrots, potatoes, and celery. Cook until softened, about 5 to 7 minutes. Add seasonings, herbs, and 1-1/2 cups broth. Blend flour into remaining stock; stir into hot vegetable mixture. Bring to a boil and simmer 8 to 10 minutes, stirring until thickened. Remove bay leaf. Stir in peas and turkey.

Spoon into pie shell. Fit second pie shell over the top and seal edges. Cut vents in center for steam to escape. Brush top pastry with milk. Bake at 400° for 10 minutes. Immediately reduce oven temperature to 350° and bake for 20 to 25 minutes or until the pastry is golden brown and filling is bubbly.

This recipe used by permission of the National Turkey Federation.

Turkey Hash Au Gratin

1/2 pound ground turkey
1 cup onion, chopped
2 cups cooked potatoes
1/2 teaspoon salt
1/4 teaspoon pepper
1/2 cup cheddar cheese

In a medium skillet, over medium-high heat, combine turkey and onions. Cook 5 minutes or until turkey is no longer pink. Add potato, breaking up larger pieces of potato with spoon if necessary; cook 2 to 3 minutes. Add salt and pepper. In a casserole, lightly coated with vegetable cooking spray, bake turkey mixture at 375° for 10 to 15 minutes. Top casserole with cheese and continue baking until cheese melts.

This recipe used by permission of the National Turkey Federation.

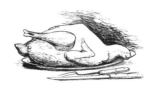

SEAFOOD

Lemon-battered Fish

1 cup flour
2/3 cup water
1/3 cup lemon juice
1 egg, beaten
1 teaspoon baking powder
1/2 teaspoon sugar
3/4 teaspoon salt
1 pound fresh or frozen fish fillets
1/3 cup lemon juice
1/2 cup flour
oil, for deep frying

Combine 1 cup flour, water, 1/3 cup lemon juice, egg, baking powder, sugar, and salt in a bowl; mix well. Dip fish in 1/3 cup lemon juice; coat with 1/2 cup flour. Dip into batter, coating well. Deep-fry in hot oil until golden brown. Makes 3 servings.

PAN-FRIED FISH

1/2 cup flour
1/2 cup cornmeal
1 tablespoon salt
1 teaspoon cayenne pepper
1/4 teaspoon dry mustard
1/2 teaspoon celery seed
1 teaspoon onion powder
1 teaspoon garlic powder
4 white fish fillets
1 cup milk
oil, for frying

In a shallow dish, combine the flour, cornmeal, salt, cayenne pepper, dry mustard, celery seed, onion powder, and garlic powder. Soak each fillet in the milk, then dredge in flour mixture. Fill a large cast iron skillet with about 1/2-inch of oil and heat to frying temperature. Fry fillets two at a time, until crispy.

BAKED OYSTERS

6 oysters
2 teaspoons butter
1/2 cup fish stock
6 ounces mayonnaise
3 ounces chili sauce
1 ounce horseradish
2 tablespoons Swiss cheese, grated

Poach oysters in the butter and stock until they curl. Drain and put back into the half shell. Combine the mayonnaise, chili sauce, and horseradish. Spread over the oysters. Sprinkle with cheese. Bake at 400° until golden brown.

BAKED SALMON

2 cups salmon
2 cups seasoned stuffing
1/2 pound cheddar cheese, grated
1/2 teaspoon salt
1/2 teaspoon dry mustard
4 eggs
2 cups milk

Drain salmon; remove bones and skin. Flake. Grease a casserole. Alternate layers of stuffing, salmon, and cheese. Mix salt and dry mustard; add eggs and beat. Stir in milk. Pour over ingredients in casserole. Bake at 325° for 1 hour.

Low Country Shrimp Boil

6 pounds smoked link sausage
30 new potatoes, unpeeled
15 ears of corn, cut into halves
10 pounds shrimp, unpeeled
1 (32-ounce) bottle ketchup
1 (12-ounce) bottle chili sauce
1 (5-ounce) jar cream-style horseradish
1/4 cup lemon juice

Cut sausage into 2 to 3-inch pieces. Combine with cold water to cover in a large saucepan. Bring to a boil over high heat. Remove a 1/4-inch strip of peel around each potato. Add potatoes to saucepan. Cook for 30 minutes; remove with slotted spoon. Cook sausage for 1 hour longer. Add corn. Cook for 10 to 15 minutes. Remove sausage and corn from saucepan. Add shrimp to boiling water in saucepan. Cook just until shrimp are pink; do not overcook. Drain shrimp and place on platters with vegetables. Combine ketchup, chili sauce, horseradish, and lemon juice in a bowl; mix well. Serve with shrimp and vegetables. Makes 30 servings.

BUTTERMILK-BATTERED FRIED SHRIMP

1-1/2 cups flour
1 teaspoon salt
1 teaspoon cayenne pepper
1-1/2 cups buttermilk
1-1/2 pounds shrimp, peeled with tails left on
vegetable oil, for frying
salt and pepper, to taste

In a large bowl, mix together the flour, salt, and cayenne pepper. Soak the shrimp in the buttermilk then dip in the batter, and fry in hot oil until golden brown, about 2 to 3 minutes. Drain and season with salt and pepper.

SHRIMP AND GRITS

6 cups chicken broth
2 cups quick-cooking grits
4 tablespoons butter
1 cup cheddar cheese, shredded
2 tablespoons extra virgin olive oil
1 small onion, finely chopped
1 pound shrimp, peeled and deveined
salt and pepper, to taste

In a medium saucepan, bring the chicken broth to a boil. Stir in the grits, cover, and reduce heat to low. Simmer, stirring occasionally, until done, about 5 minutes. Stir in the butter and cheese; continue stirring until melted. Cover.

In a skillet, heat olive oil over medium heat. Add onion and cook until translucent, about 5 minutes. Season shrimp with salt and pepper and add to skillet. Cook until shrimp turn pink, about 4 to 5 minutes. Stir shrimp and onions into grits. Cook for another 10 minutes.

Marinated Shrimp

3 teaspoons sugar
3 teaspoons salt
1 teaspoon dry mustard
3 dashes hot sauce
4 tablespoons Worcestershire sauce
1/2 cup ketchup
2/3 cup vinegar
2/3 cup vegetable oil
5 pounds shrimp, boiled and peeled
2 large onions, sliced
1 bay leaf

In a mixing bowl, combine sugar, salt, dry mustard, hot sauce, Worcestershire sauce, ketchup, vinegar, and vegetable oil. Layer shrimp, onion, and bay leaf in a 1-gallon wide mouthed jar. Pour mixture over it. Seal and let stand in refrigerator 24 hours before serving. Turn upside down every day.

OYSTER PO'BOYS

1 egg, lightly beaten
1/2 cup milk
1 teaspoon salt
1 teaspoon pepper
1-1/2 cups cornmeal
1-1/2 cups all-purpose flour
3 teaspoons paprika
3 teaspoons dried thyme
1 teaspoon cayenne pepper
vegetable oil, for frying
3 dozen oysters, shucked and drained
1 loaf French bread
3/4 cup mayonnaise
2 cups lettuce, thinly sliced
hot sauce, to taste

In a bowl, mix together the egg, milk, 1/2 teaspoon salt, and 1 teaspoon pepper. In a shallow dish, combine cornmeal, flour, paprika, thyme, 1/2 teaspoon salt, and cayenne pepper.

In a large cast iron skillet, heat vegetable oil. In batches, soak the oysters in the egg mixture, dredge them in the flour mixture, and fry in oil. Fry until golden brown, about 45 seconds to 1 minute. Drain.

Meanwhile, cut the bread into serving size pieces and toast in a warm oven, about 5 minutes. Spread mayonnaise over bread and cover with lettuce. Add fried oysters and top with hot sauce

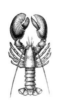

FRIED ALLIGATOR

1/4 cup all-purpose flour
1 cup cornmeal
1 tablespoon garlic powder
1 teaspoon cayenne pepper
1 teaspoon paprika
1 teaspoon salt
1 teaspoon black pepper
2 pounds alligator meat, cut into bite-sized pieces
vegetable oil, for frying

In a shallow dish, combine flour, cornmeal, garlic powder, cayenne pepper, paprika, salt, and black pepper. Dredge alligator pieces in flour mixture and fry in hot oil until golden brown, about 2 to 3 minutes.

CRAB CAKES

3 tablespoons butter
1 small onion, chopped
1/4 cup red bell pepper, finely chopped
1 garlic clove, minced
2 cups bread crumbs
1/4 cup mayonnaise
2 eggs, beaten
1 teaspoon salt
1/2 teaspoon pepper
1/2 teaspoon cayenne pepper
1 pound lump crab meat, picked over
2 tablespoons vegetable oil

In a saucepan, melt butter over medium heat. Add the onion, bell pepper, and garlic; sauté for 2 minutes. Remove from heat. Pour into a mixing bowl. Add bread crumbs, mayonnaise, eggs, and seasonings. Stir to combine. Gently fold in crab meat. Form into cakes about 1/2-inch thick and refrigerate until firm, about 2 hours. In a heavy cast iron skillet, heat vegetable oil over medium heat. Fry crab cakes until browned, about 3 minutes per side.

FRIED CATFISH

4 (6-ounce) catfish fillets
seasoning salt and pepper, to taste
1/4 cup flour
3/4 cup yellow cornmeal
1/2 teaspoon salt
vegetable oil

Sprinkle seasoning salt and pepper over each fillet. In a large bowl, combine the flour, cornmeal, and salt. Dredge the catfish in the flour mixture and fry in hot oil until golden brown, about 7 minutes. Makes 4 servings.

SALMON LOAF

1 cup canned salmon, drained
1 cup bread, cubed
1 egg, beaten
2 teaspoons salt
black pepper
1/4 cup onion, finely chopped
1/2 cup milk

Mix all ingredients well. Shape into a loaf. Bake in a casserole dish about 35 minutes at 300°.

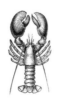

SALMON CROQUETTES

1 can pink salmon
1 bell pepper, cut into strips
1 egg
salt and pepper, to taste

Combine all ingredients and fry in a skillet until both sides are brown.

SHRIMP CREOLE

2 tablespoons vegetable oil
1 tablespoon flour
1 green bell pepper, chopped
1 onion, chopped
1 garlic clove
4 tablespoons tomato paste
pinch of red pepper
1 pound shrimp, peeled and deveined
2 cups water
salt and pepper, to taste
cooked rice

Heat oil and add flour. Cook until light brown. Add green pepper, onion, garlic, tomato paste, and red pepper. Add shrimp and water, season with salt and pepper. Cook until shrimp turn pink. Serve over rice.

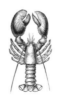

SCALLOPED OYSTERS

1/2 cup dry bread crumbs
1 cup cracker crumbs
1/2 cup butter, melted
1 container oysters, drained
1/2 cup celery, chopped
6 tablespoons cream of oyster liquor
salt
paprika
pepper
2 tablespoons parsley, chopped

Combine the bread and cracker crumbs and pour butter over them. Place a thin layer (about 1/3 of the mixture) of crumbs along the bottom of a casserole. On top of the crumbs, place a layer of oysters and celery; pour a little oyster liquor over the oysters and season. Continue layering in this fashion; ending with a layer of crumbs. Sprinkle parsley on top and bake at 400° for 20 minutes.

TUNA CASSEROLE

1 (12-ounce) can tuna
1 (8-ounce) package spaghetti noodles, cooked
1 (13-1/4-ounce) can sliced mushrooms, drained
1 (15-ounce) can English peas
1 (10-1/2-ounce) can cream of mushroom soup
1 small package potato chips

Layer tuna, pasta, mushrooms, and peas in a greased casserole. Pour soup over layers. Top with crumbled potato chips. Bake at 400° for 20 minutes.

CRAB AND SHRIMP CASSEROLE

1 pound crab meat
1 pound shrimp, cooked, peeled, and deveined
1/2 cup green bell pepper, chopped
1 tablespoon Worcestershire sauce
1 cup mayonnaise
1/4 cup onion, diced
1/4 cup celery, diced
1/2 teaspoon salt

Combine all ingredients and put into a buttered casserole. Bake at 400° for 20 minutes. Makes 6 servings.

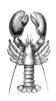

BREAKFAST
FOODS

EGG AND SAUSAGE CASSEROLE

6 eggs, beaten
1/8 teaspoon dry mustard
pinch salt
pepper to taste
2 cups milk
1 pound sausage, browned and drained
1 pound cheddar cheese, grated
6 slices white bread, crust removed and cubed

Beat eggs, add spices, then milk, sausage, cheese, and bread. Pour into a buttered casserole pan. Bake for 40 minutes.

COUNTRY PANCAKES

2 cups buttermilk
2 eggs, separated
2 teaspoons butter, melted
1 teaspoon salt
2 tablespoons sugar
2 cups flour, sifted
2 tablespoons baking soda

In a bowl, blend buttermilk, egg yolks, and melted butter. Beat egg whites until stiff but not dry. Fold gently into batter. Add salt, sugar, flour, and baking soda. Fry 4-inch cakes on hot griddle, turning once. Serve with Strawberry Cream.

Strawberry Cream

1/2 cup sour cream
1/2 cup whipping cream
2 tablespoons sugar
sliced strawberries
squeeze of lemon or lime juice

Pour sour cream and whipping cream into bowl. Beat until soft peaks form. Beat in sugar. Fold in berries and lemon juice. Serve on pancakes or waffles.

Cheese Grits

6 cups chicken broth
2 cups grits
2 eggs, beaten
1/3 cup milk
1 teaspoon salt
1 teaspoon garlic powder
1 cup cheddar cheese, grated
1/4 cup butter, softened

In a large saucepan, bring chicken broth to a boil. Stir in grits and whisk until all water is absorbed. Add the eggs, milk, salt, and garlic powder to the saucepan; mix well. Add cheese and butter; stir until melted. Pour mixture into a greased casserole and bake at 350° for 30 to 35 minutes, or until set.

DELICIOUS SOUTHERN SAUSAGE GRAVY

1 cup breakfast sausage
2 tablespoons shortening
3 tablespoons flour
1-1/2 cups milk
salt and pepper, to taste
dash cayenne pepper, optional

Cook sausage in a medium skillet over medium-low heat, stirring and breaking up with a spatula. With a slotted spoon, remove the browned crumbled sausage to a paper towel-lined plate. Add 2 tablespoons shortening to the drippings in the skillet. Add flour, stirring until blended and bubbling. Gradually add 1-1/2 cups milk; continue stirring and cooking until thickened and bubbly. Add the crumbled sausage. If too thick, add a little more milk. Taste and add salt and pepper. Stir in a dash of cayenne pepper, if desired. Serve over hot split and buttered biscuits. Makes 4 to 6 servings.

WAFFLES

1-1/2 cups flour, sifted
2 teaspoons baking powder
1/2 teaspoon salt
2 eggs, separated
1 cup milk
2 tablespoons butter, melted

Sift the dry ingredients together. Beat the egg yolks and combine the with the milk and melted butter; add gradually to dry ingredients, stirring only until the batter is smooth. Fold in beaten egg whites. Bake in a hot waffle iron.

CAKES

MISSISSIPPI MUD CAKE

2 cups sugar
1 cup butter
4 eggs
1/2 cup cocoa
1-1/2 cups pecans, chopped
1-1/2 cups plain flour
dash of salt
1 teaspoon vanilla
miniature marshmallows
icing

Cream sugar and butter together. Add eggs and blend well. Add cocoa, chopped pecans, flour, salt, and vanilla; mix well. Pour into a greased and floured pan. Bake at 350° for 35 minutes. When cake is done immediately cover the top of the cake with miniature marshmallows. Do not remove cake from pan. Pour icing over marshmallows after the cake cools.

RED VELVET CAKE

1-1/2 cups sugar
1-1/2 cups cooking oil
3 eggs
2-1/2 cups plain flour
1 teaspoon soda
2 tablespoons cocoa
2 teaspoons vanilla
2 teaspoons vinegar
1 ounce red food coloring
1 cup buttermilk

Cream sugar and oil; add eggs. Mix flour, soda, and cocoa with sifter. Add vanilla, vinegar, and food coloring to sugar mixture. Add flour alternating with milk. Bake in 3 layers at 300° for 30 minutes. Do not overcook. Ice with Cream Cheese Frosting.

CREAM CHEESE FROSTING

1 (16-ounce) box powdered sugar
1/2 cup margarine
1 (8-ounce) package cream cheese
1 small can coconut
1 cup nuts, chopped

Mix all ingredients and spread on cooled cake.

APPLESAUCE CAKE

1/2 cup shortening
1 cup brown sugar
1 cup applesauce
2-1/4 cups flour
1/2 teaspoon baking soda
1/2 teaspoon salt
1 teaspoon baking powder
1/2 teaspoon cloves
1/2 teaspoon cinnamon
1/4 teaspoon nutmeg
1 cup walnuts

Cream shortening and sugar. Add applesauce. Add dry ingredients and beat. Add walnuts. Pour into a greased loaf pan. Bake at 325° for 1 hour.

OLD-FASHIONED SOUTHERN TEA CAKES

2-1/4 cups all purpose flour, sifted
1 cup sugar
1/2 cup melted butter
1-1/2 teaspoons vanilla
1 egg

Mix all ingredients until moist. Roll dough on floured surface and cut tea cakes to desired size. Bake at 350° until done (depending on degree of thickness).

CHERRY CAKE

1 package devil's food cake
1 teaspoon almond extract
1 (21-ounce) cherry pie filling
3 eggs

Combine all ingredients and mix well. Pour into a greased tube pan. Bake at 350° for 55 minutes or until done. Let cool in pan.

CARROT CAKE

1-1/2 cups cooking oil
2 cups sugar
4 eggs
2 cups flour, sifted
2 teaspoons baking powder
1-1/2 teaspoons soda
1 teaspoon salt
2 teaspoons cinnamon
2 cups carrots, grated
1/2 cup nuts
1 small can crushed pineapple, drained
1/2 cup butter
1 (8-ounce) package cream cheese
1 teaspoon vanilla
1 (16-ounce) box powdered sugar

Mix oil, sugar, and eggs. Beat well. Add sifted dry ingredients and beat. Add carrots, nuts, and pineapple. Bake in 3 greased and floured layer pans at 350° for 30 minutes.

For the icing, cream butter and cream cheese together. Add vanilla and powdered sugar. Spread on top of cake.

Chess Cake

1 box yellow cake mix
1/2 cup butter
4 eggs
1 (8-ounce) package cream cheese
1 (16-ounce) box powdered sugar

Mix cake mix, butter, and 1 egg and press in the bottom of oblong pan. Mix cream cheese, 3 eggs, and powdered sugar and pour over the first mixture. Bake at 350° for 30 to 35 minutes or until lightly brown on top.

Coconut Cake

1 box yellow or white cake mix
1 can sweetened condensed milk
1 can cream of coconut
1 large container of whipped cream topping
2 cups coconut

Bake cake according to directions on the box. While still warm, prick with fork. Mix milk and cream of coconut and spread over cake. When cool, cover with whipped cream topping and sprinkle with coconut.

FRESH APPLE CAKE

1 cup cooking oil
2 cups sugar
2 eggs
2 teaspoons vanilla
3 cups flour
1/2 teaspoon salt
1 teaspoon soda
3 cups apples, chopped
1 cup walnuts or pecans, chopped

Combine oil and sugar. Add eggs and vanilla. Measure and sift together flour, salt, and soda. Add dry ingredients to first mixture. Stir in chopped fresh apples and nuts. Mix thoroughly. Place in a greased pan. Bake at 325° about 45 minutes.

HUMMINGBIRD CAKE

3 cups all-purpose flour
2 cups sugar
1 teaspoon salt
1 teaspoon baking soda
1 teaspoon cinnamon
3 eggs
1-1/2 cups oil
1-1/2 teaspoons vanilla
1 (8-ounce) can crushed pineapple, undrained
2 cups pecans or walnuts, chopped
2 cups bananas, mashed
2 (8-ounce) packages cream cheese
1 cup butter
2 (16-ounce) boxes powdered sugar
2 teaspoons vanilla

Combine dry ingredients in a large bowl. Add eggs and oil, stirring until dry ingredients are moistened. Do not beat. Stir in vanilla, pineapple and 1 cup chopped nuts and bananas, and spoon into three well greased and floured 9-inch cake pans. Bake at 350° for 25 to 30 minutes, until cake tests done. Cool in pans 10 minutes. Remove from pans and cool completely.

Meanwhile, combine softened cream cheese and butter. Cream until smooth. Add powdered sugar. Beat until light and fluffy. Stir in vanilla.

Spread cream cheese frosting between layers of cake and on top and sides. Sprinkle with remaining 1 cup nuts.

PINEAPPLE UPSIDE-DOWN CAKE

1/2 cup butter
1 cup brown sugar
1 (21-ounce) can sliced pineapple
12 maraschino cherries, halved
1 cup pecans, chopped
1 package yellow cake mix

Melt butter and sugar in a cake pan in a 375° oven; remove and spread evenly. Arrange pineapple, cherries, and nuts. Mix cake according to directions and spread in pan. Bake according to directions.

POUND CAKE

1 cup margarine or butter
1/2 cup shortening
3 cups sugar
5 eggs
3-1/4 cups plain flour
1/2 teaspoon baking powder
1/2 teaspoon salt
1 cup milk
1 teaspoon vanilla

Beat butter and shortening until very light and fluffy. Add sugar gradually and beat well. Add eggs, one at a time and beat well. Sift flour, baking powder, and salt and add by spoonfuls alternately with milk. Add vanilla. Bake at 325° for almost 2 hours. If you prefer chocolate cake, reduce flour by 1/4 cup and add 1/4 cup cocoa.

CINNAMON COFFEE CAKE

2 cups buttermilk baking mix
2/3 cup milk
2 tablespoons sugar
2 tablespoons cinnamon
1 egg
1/3 cup baking mix
1/3 cup brown sugar
1/2 teaspoon cinnamon
2 tablespoons butter

In a large bowl, combine the 2 cups baking mix with the milk, sugar, 2 tablespoons cinnamon, and egg. Beat for 1 minute. Spread batter into a buttered baking dish. Mix together the 1/3 cup baking mix, brown sugar, 1/2 teaspoon cinnamon, and butter. Mix until crumbly. Sprinkle over batter. Bake at 350° for 18 to 22 minutes.

SNAPDOODLE

1/2 cup shortening
1 cup sugar
3 cups all-purpose flour
1/2 teaspoon salt
1 teaspoon baking powder
1-1/2 cups milk
1-1/2 cups brown sugar, packed
1/8 teaspoon cinnamon
1/8 teaspoon mace

Combine shortening and sugar in a mixing bowl, and cream until the mixture is fluffy. In another mixing bowl, combine the flour, salt, and baking powder. Add the flour mixture to the sugar mixture alternately with the milk, and mix well. Pour the batter into a buttered baking pan. Combine the brown sugar, cinnamon, and mace in a small bowl. Mix well and sprinkle over the top of the batter. Bake at 350° until brown, about 50 minutes. After it cools, cut into squares.

ORANGE CAKE

1 cup butter
2 cups sugar
1 teaspoon orange peel, grated
4 eggs
1 teaspoon baking soda
4 cups flour
1-1/3 cups buttermilk
1 package dates, finely chopped
1 cup pecans, finely chopped
2 cups sugar
1 cup orange juice
2 teaspoons orange peel, grated

Cream the butter thoroughly. Add sugar slowly until it is well blended with the butter. Beat orange rind into the mixture. Add eggs one at a time, beating after each addition. Sift the dry ingredients together. Add dry ingredients to the mixture alternately with the milk. Next add dates and pecans, beating until well blended.

Pour the batter into a well-greased tube pan. Bake at 325° for 1-1/2 hours.

For orange sauce, combine 2 cups sugar, 1 cup orange juice, and 2 teaspoons grated orange peel; stir until dissolved. Remove cake from oven and pour orange sauce over it while it is still in the pan. Allow cake to cool before removing from pan.

CARAMEL CAKE

2 cups sugar
1 cup butter
4 eggs
2-1/2 cups flour
1-1/2 teaspoons baking powder
1/4 teaspoon salt
1 cup milk
1 teaspoon vanilla

Cream sugar and butter. Add eggs, one at a time, beating after each addition. Sift flour with baking powder and salt. Add dry ingredients to the batter, alternating with milk. Add vanilla. Bake in three greased and floured cake pans for 25 minutes at 350°.

FRUIT CAKE

1 pound candied cherries
1 box raisins
1-1/2 pounds walnuts
1-1/2 pounds pecans
1/2 pound candied pineapple
1 pound package orange slice candy
1 pound miniature marshmallows
1 can sweetened condensed milk
1 small box vanilla wafers or graham crackers

Chop fruits and nuts. Slice orange candy. Melt marshmallows in a double boiler. Add milk and vanilla wafers to melted marshmallows, but do not stir. Add fruit, nuts, and candy. Stir well. Press batter into a greased tube pan. Cover tightly with foil. Refrigerate over night. Serve chilled.

Cocoa Cheesecake

2 (8-ounce) packages cream cheese
3/4 cup sugar
1/2 cup cocoa
1 teaspoon vanilla
2 eggs
graham cracker pie shell
1 cup sour cream
2 tablespoons sugar
1 teaspoon vanilla

Beat cream cheese, 3/4 cup sugar, cocoa, and 1 teaspoon vanilla until light and fluffy. Add eggs, blend well. Pour into pie shell. Bake at 375° for 20 minutes. Remove from oven and cool for 15 minutes.

Combine sour cream, 2 tablespoons sugar, and 1 teaspoon vanilla; stir until smooth. Spread evenly over cake. Bake at 425° for 10 minutes. Chill several hours or overnight.

Turtle Cake

1 box German chocolate cake mix
1 (14-ounce) package caramel candies
1 small can evaporated milk
3/4 cup butter
1 cup pecans
1 cup chocolate chips

Prepare cake mix according to package directions. Pour half of the batter into a greased and floured baking pan. Bake at 350° for 15 minutes. In top of a double boiler, melt together the caramel candies, milk, and butter. Pour this over the cake. Sprinkle the pecans and chocolate chips over the caramel mixture. Spread remaining batter over caramel mixture. Bake an additional 25 to 30 minutes.

Brown Sugar Spice Cake

1-1/2 cups flour
1/4 teaspoon salt
2-1/2 teaspoons baking powder
1/2 teaspoon cinnamon
1/2 teaspoon cloves
1/2 teaspoon allspice
1/2 cup shortening
1 cup brown sugar
2 egg yolks
1/2 cup milk
1/2 teaspoon vanilla

Sift together the flour, salt, baking powder, cinnamon, cloves, and allspice. Cream shortening and sugar; beat in egg yolks. Stir in dry ingredients alternately with milk and vanilla. Spread batter in a greased baking pan. Bake at 350° for 35 minutes.

DEPRESSION CAKE

1 cup brown sugar
1-1/4 cups water
1/3 cup shortening
2/3 cup raisins
1/2 teaspoon nutmeg
2 teaspoons cinnamon
1/2 teaspoon cloves
1 teaspoon salt
2 teaspoons baking soda
2 cups flour
1 teaspoon baking powder

Boil sugar, water, shortening, raisins, and spices together for 3 minutes. Cool; add salt and soda dissolved in 2 teaspoons water. Gradually add flour and baking powder sifted together, beating until smooth after each addition. Bake in a greased pan at 325° for 50 minutes.

COOKIES

Peanut Butter Cookies

1 cup butter
1-1/2 cups crunchy peanut butter
1-1/2 cups dark brown sugar
2/3 cup sugar
2 eggs
2 teaspoons vanilla
2-2/3 cups plain flour
2 teaspoons baking soda

Cream butter, peanut butter, and sugars well. Add eggs and vanilla. Sift the flour and soda together and add creamed mixture. Mix well. Shape into small balls about 1-inch in size. Place on a cookie sheet. Bake at 350° for 10 minutes. Makes about 12 dozen cookies.

Sugar Cookies

1 cup butter
1 cup oil
2 eggs
1 cup sugar
1 cup powdered sugar
4-1/2 cups plain flour
1 teaspoon baking soda
1 teaspoon cream of tartar
1 teaspoon vanilla

Mix butter, oil, eggs, and sugar. Add all other dry ingredients gradually. Add vanilla. Roll into walnut-sized balls. Flatten with a fork. Sprinkle lightly with sugar. Bake at 350° for 10 to 12 minutes.

GINGERBREAD COOKIES

1 cup shortening
1 cup brown sugar
1-1/2 cups molasses
1/2 cup hot water
2 eggs
6 cups flour
2 teaspoons baking soda
1 tablespoon ginger
1 teaspoon cinnamon
1 teaspoon ground cloves
1 teaspoon allspice
2-1/2 cups powdered sugar
2 egg whites
1/2 teaspoon cream of tartar
lemon juice
peppermint extract, to taste

Mix shortening, brown sugar, and molasses together until smooth. Stir in hot water and mix well. Beat in eggs. Sift flour, baking soda, ginger, cinnamon, cloves, and allspice together. Add dry mixture slowly to the shortening mixture, making smooth dough. Chill dough in a floured bowl for 1 hour. Toss on floured board. Roll to 1/2-inch thickness. Cut with cookie cutters. Place cookies on greased cookie sheet and bake at 375° for 10 to 15 minutes, until edges are brown.

Meanwhile, beat the powdered sugar, egg whites, cream of tartar, lemon juice, and peppermint extract at high speed until icing holds a point. Cover bowl with damp cloth until ready to use. Top cookies with icing.

OLD-FASHIONED BUTTER COOKIES

1/2 pound butter
1 cup sugar
1 egg
1 teaspoon vanilla
2 cups flour

Cream butter and sugar. Add egg and vanilla. Gradually add flour. Drop by teaspoon on cookie sheet. Flatten with fork. Bake about 10 minutes at 350° or until brown.

SNICKERDOODLES

1 cup shortening
1-1/2 cups sugar
2 eggs
2 tablespoons milk
1 teaspoon vanilla
2-3/4 cups all-purpose flour
2 teaspoons cream of tartar
1 teaspoon baking soda
3/4 teaspoon salt
1/2 cup sugar
2 teaspoons cinnamon

Cream shortening, 1-1/2 cups sugar, eggs, milk, and vanilla in a large bowl until well blended. Combine flour, cream of tartar, baking soda, and salt. Mix into creamed mixture. Shape dough into 1-inch balls. Combine 1/2 cup sugar and cinnamon in a small bowl. Roll balls of dough in mixture. Place 2 inches apart on an ungreased baking sheet. Bake at 400° for 7 to 8 minutes. Remove to cooling rack.

HAYSTACKS

1/4 cup butter
1/2 cup creamy peanut butter
1 (12-ounce) package butterscotch chips
6 cups corn cereal
2/3 cups miniature semisweet chocolate

Melt butter, peanut butter, and butterscotch chips in a large saucepan over very low heat. Stir constantly until melted. Remove from heat. Pour corn cereal into a large bowl. Pour hot butterscotch mixture over cereal. Stir with large spoon until cereal is coated. Stir in chocolate chips. Spoon out mixture into mounds on wax paper-lined baking sheets. Refrigerate until firm before serving. Makes 3 dozen 2-1/2-inch cookies.

HERMIT COOKIES

1 cup shortening
2 cups brown sugar
2 eggs, well beaten
3-1/2 cups flour
1/2 teaspoon salt
1 teaspoon baking powder
1 teaspoon baking soda
2 teaspoons cinnamon
1 teaspoon nutmeg
1/2 cup milk
2 cups raisins
1 cup pecans, chopped

Thoroughly cream shortening and brown sugar. Add eggs and beat well. Add sifted dry ingredients alternately with milk. Add raisins and pecans. Drop from teaspoon onto a greased cookie sheet. Bake at 375° for about 15 minutes. Makes 4 dozen cookies.

OATMEAL COOKIES

2 cups brown sugar
1/2 cup butter, melted
2 eggs, well beaten
1-1/2 teaspoons vanilla
1 teaspoon baking soda
4 cups rolled oats
2 cups flour
1 cup coconut, shredded

Mix brown sugar and melted butter together. Add eggs and vanilla. Mix soda, oats, flour, and coconut together and add to the first mixture. Form two 2-inch rolls, wrap in wax paper. Cool in refrigerator for 4 to 5 hours. Slice thin and bake at 350° for 12 to 15 minutes, or until browned.

FROZEN COOKIES

1 cup brown sugar
1 cup white sugar
3/4 cup butter
1 cup vegetable shortening
3 eggs, well beaten
1 teaspoon salt
1 teaspoon baking soda
1 teaspoon cinnamon
1 teaspoon cloves

Cream sugars, butter, and shortening. Add eggs and beat well. Mix and sift dry ingredients; add to the first mixture, mixing well. Work dough into a long round roll. Freeze for about 3 hours. Slice thin and place on a greased cookie sheet. Bake at 400° for 7 minutes, or until done.

Vanilla Cookies

2 eggs
2/3 cup oil
3/4 cup sugar
2 teaspoons vanilla
2 cups self-rising flour

Beat eggs until fluffy. Add oil, sugar, and vanilla. Add flour gradually and mix well. Drop by spoonfuls on a cookie sheet. Bake at 350° until lightly browned.

Pecan Squares

1-1/4 cups biscuit mix
3 eggs
1-1/2 cups brown sugar
3/4 cup pecans, chopped
powdered sugar

Blend all ingredients except powdered sugar until just moistened. Spread mixture into a greased baking pan. Bake at 350° for 20 to 25 minutes. Cool. Cut into 2-inch squares and sprinkle with powdered sugar.

NOELS

1 cup margarine
1/2 cup powdered sugar
2 teaspoons vanilla
2 cups flour
1 cup nuts, chopped

Cream together margarine and powdered sugar. Add remaining ingredients. Mix well. Shape into small balls and bake at 350° for 20 minutes.

ALMOND COOKIES

1/2 cup butter, softened
1/2 cup shortening
1 cup powdered sugar
1 egg
1-1/2 teaspoons almond extract
1 teaspoon vanilla
2-1/2 cups flour
1 teaspoon salt

Cream the butter, shortening, sugar, egg, almond extract, and vanilla together. Blend in flour and salt. Form into 60 balls and place on a cookie sheet. Bake at 375° for 10 to 12 minutes.

BUTTERSCOTCH PINWHEELS

1 (6-ounce) semisweet chocolate chips
2 tablespoons shortening
1/2 cup milk
1 cup all-purpose flour, sifted
1 teaspoon vanilla
1 (6-ounce) package butterscotch morsels
2 tablespoons shortening
1/2 cup nuts, chopped

Melt chocolate chips and shortening in top of a double boiler over boiling water. Remove from heat. Add milk, flour, and vanilla; blend well. Spread out onto a wax-paper lined cookie sheet. Bake at 325° for 8 minutes.

Meanwhile, melt the butterscotch morsels and shortening in the top of a double boiler over boiling water.

Spread filling across chocolate base and sprinkle with nuts. Roll up, wrap, and chill for 6 hours. Cut into slices. Makes 5 dozen cookies.

OLD-FASHIONED CHOCOLATE CHIP COOKIES

2/3 cup shortening
2/3 cup butter
1 cup white sugar
1 cup brown sugar
2 eggs
2 teaspoons vanilla
3 cups self-rising flour
1 (12-ounce) package semisweet chocolate chips

Mix the shortening, butter, sugars, eggs, and vanilla thoroughly. Sift in the flour and add the chocolate chips. Stir to combine. Drop by spoonfuls onto an ungreased cookie sheet. Bake at 350° for 8 to 10 minutes, or until light brown.

PECAN COOKIES

1 cup brown sugar, packed
1-1/2 cups white sugar
1 pound margarine
3 eggs, beaten
5 cups all-purpose flour
1/2 teaspoon salt
1 teaspoon baking soda
4 cups pecan pieces

Cream together the sugars and margarine. Add eggs and mix well. Sift the flour, salt, and baking powder together and add to the margarine. Stir in nuts. Roll into 3 long rolls and wrap in wax paper. Refrigerate overnight. Slice and bake at 350° for about 10 to 15 minutes.

PIES

PUMPKIN PIE

1 (16-ounce) can solid pack pumpkin
1 (12-ounce) can evaporated skim milk
2 large eggs
2/3 cup sugar
2 teaspoons pumpkin pie spice
1 (9-inch) pie shell

In large bowl combine pumpkin, milk, eggs, sugar, and pumpkin pie spice. Pour into pie shell. Bake at 425° for 15 minutes. Reduce oven to 350° and continue to bake another 40 to 50 minutes or until knife inserted in center comes out clean.

This recipe used by permission of the National Turkey Federation.

SWEET POTATO PIE

2 cups sweet potatoes, cooked and mashed
1 cup sugar
1/2 teaspoon salt
1 cup milk
2 eggs, beaten
1 tablespoon butter, melted
1 teaspoon vanilla
dash of nutmeg

Mix all ingredients. Pour into unbaked pie shell. Bake at 350° for 35 to 45 minutes or until firm.

LEMON ICE BOX PIE

3 eggs, separated
1 cup sweetened condensed milk
juice of 2 lemons
vanilla wafers
2 tablespoons sugar

Beat egg yolks and mix with milk. Add lemon juice, stirring well. Pour into pie pan lined with vanilla wafers. Beat the egg whites until stiff, add sugar, and spread on pie. Bake at 350° until brown. Chill in refrigerator.

FRESH BLUEBERRY CREAM PIE

1 cup sour cream
2 tablespoons all-purpose flour
3/4 cup sugar
1/4 teaspoon salt
1 egg, beaten
1 teaspoon vanilla
2-1/2 cups fresh blueberries
1 (9-inch) unbaked pastry shell
3 tablespoons all-purpose flour
3 tablespoons margarine or butter, softened
3 tablespoons pecans or walnuts, chopped

Combine first six ingredients; beat 5 minutes at medium speed of electric mixer or until smooth. Fold in blueberries, pour into shell, and bake at 400° for 25 minutes. Combine remaining ingredients, stirring well; sprinkle over top of pie and bake 10 more minutes. Chill before serving.

FRESH STRAWBERRY PIE

1 quart fresh strawberries
1 cup sugar
1/2 teaspoon salt
2 tablespoons cornstarch
1/2 cup boiling water
red food coloring
1 baked pie shell
1/2 pint whipping cream

Wash, hull, and sort berries. Mash or crush enough berries to make 1 cup. Mix sugar, salt, cornstarch, crushed berries, and boiling water. Cook stirring constantly until thick, add food coloring, and cool. Just before serving, place whole berries in pie shell, pour cooled sauce over berries, and garnish with whipping cream.

FUDGE PIE

1/2 cup butter
3 tablespoons cocoa
1 cup sugar
2 eggs, beaten
1/2 cup plain flour, sifted
1/2 cup pecans, chopped
1 teaspoon vanilla

In a saucepan, melt butter and cocoa together. Mix in sugar and then remaining ingredients. Pour into pie plate. Bake at 350° for 25 to 30 minutes. Serve warm.

SOUTHERN PECAN PIE

1 cup sugar
1/2 cup dark corn syrup
1/4 cup margarine, melted
3 eggs, well beaten
1 cup pecans
1 (9-inch) unbaked pie shell

Combine sugar, syrup, and melted margarine. Add eggs and pecans. Mix thoroughly. Pour into the buttered pie shell and bake at 375° for 40 to 45 minutes.

PEANUT BUTTER PIE

3/4 cup powdered sugar
1/3 cup peanut butter
2/3 cup sugar
3 tablespoons cornstarch
1 tablespoon flour
1/2 teaspoon salt
3 cups sweet milk
2 tablespoons butter
1 teaspoon vanilla
3 eggs, separated
1 (9-inch) pie shell
1/4 teaspoon cream of tartar
1/4 cup white sugar

Cream powdered sugar and peanut butter (it will be crumbly) and set mixture aside. In a saucepan, mix together sugar, cornstarch, flour, salt, milk, butter, vanilla, and egg yolks. Cook over medium heat, stirring constantly until thick. Sprinkle 2/3 of crumb mixture in bottom of the pie shell. Pour custard in pie shell over crumb mixture. Beat egg whites and cream of tartar until stiff, adding the 1/4 cup sugar slowly; spread over custard. Sprinkle remainder of peanut butter mix over top of meringue. Bake at 350° until brown.

RAISIN NUT PIE

1 cup raisins
3/4 cup boiling water
1/2 cup sugar
2 tablespoons flour
1/4 teaspoon salt
1/2 cup orange juice
1/2 cup lemon juice
1/2 cup nuts, chopped
1/4 cup butter
1 (9-inch) pie shell
milk

Cook raisins in boiling water for 5 minutes. Mix sugar, flour, and salt together; add to raisin and water mixture. Cook until thick, then remove from heat and add juices. Let cool. Stir in nuts and pour into pie shell. Dot with butter. Cover with top crust and brush with milk. Bake at 450° until pie starts to brown. Reduce heat to 350° and finish baking.

WILD ELDERBERRY PIE

2 cups elderberries
1 tablespoon lemon juice
3/4 cup sugar
1/4 teaspoon salt
2 tablespoons flour
1 tablespoon butter
1 (9-inch) pie shell

Combine the elderberries, lemon juice, sugar, salt, and flour. Fill pie shell with elderberry mixture and dot with butter. Arrange strips of pastry over the top to form lattice. Crimp edges. Bake at 400° for 40 to 50 minutes. Makes 6 servings.

CHOCOLATE PIE

3 cups sugar
1 teaspoon cornstarch
1-1/2 teaspoons flour
dash of salt
2 eggs, beaten
2 squares bitter chocolate, melted
1/4 cup margarine
1 large can evaporated milk
1 teaspoon vanilla
1-1/2 cups coconut
1-1/2 cups pecans, chopped
2 unbaked pie shells

Mix dry ingredients, add eggs. Add chocolate and margarine. Stir in milk and add vanilla. Divide the coconut and pecans evenly between the two pie shells. Pour in filling. Bake at 350° for 40 minutes.

BUTTERMILK PIE

1-1/2 cups sugar
1/2 cup butter
3 eggs
2 tablespoons flour
1 teaspoon vanilla
1/2 cup buttermilk
1 unbaked pie shell

Beat sugar and butter; add eggs, flour, and vanilla. Beat well and add butter milk. Pour into the pie shell. Bake at 350° for 35 to 40 minutes, or until firm. Makes 8 servings.

BUTTERSCOTCH PIE

1 cup brown sugar
1 tablespoon butter
2 cups milk
2 eggs
2 tablespoons flour
dash of salt
vanilla
1 (9-inch) baked pie shell

Combine brown sugar and butter in a skillet. Cook until caramelized. Combine milk, eggs, flour, salt, and vanilla. Pour into skillet with caramelized sugar. Pour into the baked crust and bake at 350° for 15 to 20 minutes, or until golden brown.

LEMON MERINGUE PIE

1 cup sugar
3 tablespoons cornstarch
3 egg yolks
1 teaspoon margarine
1/4 cup lemon juice
1-1/2 cups water
3 egg whites
1 teaspoon water
2 tablespoons sugar
1 (9-inch) baked pie shell

Mix together the sugar, cornstarch, egg yolks, margarine, and lemon juice. Pour into a saucepan, add 1-1/2 cups of water, and bring to a boil. Pour into the pie shell.

Beat together the egg whites and water. Add the sugar and beat until smooth. Spread over pie. Bake at 425° until brown.

PEACH PIE

3 tablespoons cornstarch
1 cup sugar
1 cup boiling water
3 tablespoons peach-flavored gelatin
3 teaspoons butter
1/2 teaspoon almond extract
1 quart diced peaches
1 (9-inch) baked pie shell

Combine cornstarch and sugar. Slowly add boiling water and cook 2 minutes. Remove from heat. Add gelatin, butter, and extract. Let cool. Add peaches and pour into the pie shell. Top with whipped cream.

OTHER
DESSERTS

LEMON BARS

2 cups flour
1 cup powdered sugar
1/8 teaspoon salt
1/2 cup butter, softened
2 eggs
2 cups sugar
1/3 cup flour
juice of 1 lemon

Mix the flour, powdered sugar, and salt in a bowl. Slowly stir in butter. Pour the mixture into a greased baking dish. Bake at 350° for 20 minutes.

Whisk together the eggs, sugar, flour, and lemon juice in a bowl. Spoon mixture into the crust and bake at 300° for 30 more minutes.

BROWNIES

1/2 cup butter
1 cup sugar
2 eggs
1 teaspoon vanilla
2 squares chocolate, melted
3/4 cup flour, sifted
3/4 teaspoon salt
1/2 teaspoon baking powder
2/3 cup nuts, chopped

Cream butter, add sugar gradually, continuing to cream until mixture looks light and fluffy. Beat in eggs one at a time. Add vanilla and melted chocolate; beat well. Sift dry ingredients together and blend with chocolate mixture. Fold nuts into batter. Bake in a greased pan at 350° for 25 to 30 minutes.

BLUEBERRY COBBLER

1 tablespoon cornstarch
1/2 cup sugar
4 cups fresh blueberries
1 teaspoon lemon juice
1 cup flour
1 tablespoon sugar
1-1/2 teaspoons baking powder
1/2 teaspoon salt
3 tablespoons shortening
1/2 cup milk

Mix together cornstarch and 1/2 cup sugar in a saucepan; stir in blueberries and lemon juice and cook; stirring constantly until it thickens and boils. Cook 1 minute. Pour into casserole dish.
Mix flour, sugar, baking powder and salt; add shortening and milk and mix until dough forms. Do not stir too much. Drop dough by spoonfuls into hot berries and bake 25 to 30 minutes at 375°.

PEACH COBBLER

1-1/2 cups flour
1/2 cup shortening
1/2 teaspoon salt
1 teaspoon baking powder
1/2 cup milk
2 cups canned peaches, drained, juice reserved
1/2 cup butter, melted
2 cups sugar
water

Mix first five ingredients and roll out dough; put fruit on it and roll as jelly roll. Grease a cookie sheet with the melted butter. Place cut rolls onto cookie sheet. Mix 2 cups sugar with juice from fruit and water to make 3 cups of liquid; pour over dough. Bake at 325° for 1 hour, or until brown.

CARAMEL CORN

1 cup light brown sugar
1/4 cup light corn syrup
1/2 cup butter
1/8 teaspoon cream of tartar
1/2 teaspoon salt
1/2 teaspoon baking soda
4 quarts popcorn, popped

Cook first five ingredients over medium heat until it forms a hard ball, about 5 minutes. Remove from heat; stir in baking soda. Pour over popcorn and mix well. Bake 30 minutes at 275°; stir 2 to 3 times while baking. Remove from oven and continue stirring until partially cooled to prevent popcorn from sticking together. Store in airtight container.

PEANUT BRITTLE

2 cups sugar
1/2 cup white corn syrup
1/2 cup water
1 cup raw peanuts
pinch baking soda

Mix first three ingredients together and let come to a good boil. Add nuts and cook until they pop. Remove from heat, add baking soda and beat. Pour into a greased pan and cool.

SOUTHERN BANANA PUDDING

1 package vanilla pudding
2 eggs, separated
2-1/2 cups milk
30 to 35 vanilla wafers
2 large bananas, sliced
dash of salt
1/4 cup sugar

Combine pudding mix, egg yolks, and milk in a medium saucepan. Cook on medium heat until mixture comes to full boil, stirring constantly. Remove from heat. Arrange layer of vanilla wafers on bottom and up sides of a baking dish. Add 1 layer of banana slices; top with 1/3 of the pudding. Continue layering wafers, banana, and pudding, ending with pudding. Beat egg whites and salt with electric mixer until foamy. Gradually add sugar, beating until stiff peaks form. Spoon lightly on pudding, sealing edges well. Bake 5 to 10 minutes or until meringue is lightly browned. Serve warm or refrigerate until ready to serve. Before serving, garnish with additional vanilla wafers and banana slices, if desired. Makes 8 servings.

INDIAN PUDDING

4 cups milk
1/2 cup cornmeal
1/4 cup sugar
1/2 teaspoon cinnamon
1/4 teaspoon nutmeg
1 teaspoon salt
1 cup molasses
2 tablespoons melted butter or margarine

Scald 3 cups of the milk in the top of a double boiler. Add cornmeal, sugar, spices, salt, molasses, and butter. Cook over boiling water, stirring constantly until the mixture thickens or for about 20 minutes. Pour into a greased baking pan. Add the remaining cup of milk, without stirring. Bake at 300° for about 2-1/2 hours. Serve warm with milk or cream or ice cream. Makes 6 to 8 servings.

BANANA CREAM

1 banana, peeled and mashed
juice of 1 lemon
1 cup powdered sugar
1 cup milk
dash of salt
1 cup whipped cream

Mix pulp of mashed banana, lemon juice, powdered sugar, milk, and salt. Fold in whipped cream. Makes 1 pint.

Rich Custard

3/4 cup sugar
3 tablespoons cornstarch
pinch of salt
4 cups whole milk
2 teaspoons fresh orange zest
10 large egg yolks
1 teaspoon vanilla

Whisk together 1/4 cup sugar, cornstarch, and a pinch of salt in a 2-quart heavy saucepan. Whisk in 1/4 cup milk until smooth, then stir in remaining milk and zest. Bring to a boil over moderate heat, whisking frequently.

Have ready a bowl filled with ice and cold water. Whisk together yolks and remaining 1/2 cup sugar in a large bowl. Gradually whisk in hot milk mixture, then transfer custard to saucepan. Cook, stirring constantly, until mixture registers 170° on an instant-read thermometer, 3 to 4 minutes. (Do not boil.)

Immediately pour custard through a fine sieve into a metal bowl set in ice water. Stir in vanilla. Cool, stirring frequently. Makes 5 servings.

PEACH BREAD PUDDING

2-1/2 cups diced fresh peaches
1/4 cup peach nectar
4 to 5 cups soft bread crumbs
2 tablespoons melted butter
4 eggs
1/2 cup sugar
1-3/4 cups half-and-half or whole milk
1 teaspoon vanilla extract
1/2 cup brown sugar
2 tablespoons corn syrup
1/4 cup butter
1/2 cup heavy cream
1-1/2 teaspoons vanilla

Put diced peaches in a saucepan with peach nectar; simmer for about 5 minutes, until peaches are tender.

In a lightly buttered baking dish or rectangular baking pan, arrange bread crumbs. Drizzle bread crumbs with 2 tablespoons melted butter then toss with the peach mixture.

In a bowl, whisk eggs with sugar, milk, and 1 teaspoon vanilla. Pour mixture over bread crumbs, stirring slightly to distribute milk mixture evenly. Bake at 325° for 1 hour to 1 hour and 15 minutes, until set in center.

Meanwhile, combine the brown sugar, corn syrup, butter, heavy cream, and 1-1/2 teaspoons vanilla in a saucepan over medium heat. Bring to a boil, stirring frequently. Reduce heat to medium-low and let boil for 5 minutes. Remove from heat. Sauce will thicken as it cools. Pour over pudding.

RICE PUDDING

2 cups cooked rice
1 cup sugar
1/2 teaspoon salt
1-1/2 cups milk
1 teaspoon vanilla
1 cup raisins
2 tablespoons butter

Mix all ingredients and pour into a greased baking pan. Bake at 350°
for 25 to 30 minutes.

SOUTHERN FRIED BANANAS

1 teaspoon sweet unsalted butter
2 ripe bananas, peeled and sliced lengthwise
1 tablespoon brown sugar

In a shallow chafing dish, melt butter over medium heat. Place the
bananas in the melted butter and very gently brown on both sides,
turning gently with a wide spatula. Sprinkle brown sugar around
bananas to form a syrup. Baste continually until caramelized.

Peanut Butter Fudge

2-1/2 cups sugar
1/3 cup corn syrup
1 small can evaporated milk
2 teaspoons butter
1 teaspoon vanilla
1 large package chocolate chips
1 cup peanut butter

Mix all ingredients together except chocolate chips and peanut butter. Mix well and bring to a boil. Cook 5 minutes. Remove from heat. Add chocolate chips and peanut butter. Stir until melted. Pour into a buttered pan and chill.

Divinity

3 cups sugar
1/2 cup white corn syrup
1/2 cup cold water
2 egg whites, beaten
1 teaspoon vanilla

Bring sugar, corn syrup, and water to a boil. Cook until treads form. Pour over beaten egg whites and add vanilla. Drop on wax paper.

POTATO CANDY

1 potato, peeled
1 box powdered sugar
1 small jar peanut butter

In a saucepan, boil potato until well done and mash it. Mix in powdered sugar until it thickens. Roll out on a floured surface and spread with peanut butter. Roll up, wrap in wax paper, and refrigerate until cool enough to slice.

INDEX

C

INDEX

∼

D

INDEX

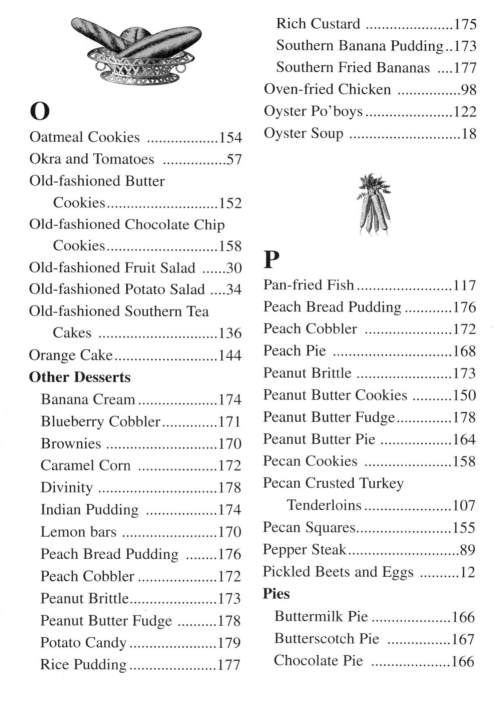

INDEX

R

S

Salads

Seafood

INDEX

INDEX

W